ELEVEN YEARS

(or Ten Paces to the Privy)

by
Wynne Broughton

Published by
Derbyshire County Council
1988

"Eleven Years Hard" is part of Derbyshire Library Service's publication programme, which is designed to bring into print material on the people, landscapes and workplaces of Derbyshire.

All proceeds from sales go towards financing the publication of further suitable texts.

Thanks are due to Mr. G. Burnham, of Chesterfield College of Technology and Art and to Mr. John Bradley for producing the front cover design and the illustrations.

ISBN 090346327X

© Winifred Broughton

DERBYSHIRE
County Council
Supports Nuclear Free Zones

Printed by: Mastaprint Limited
Derby Road Industrial Estate, Sandiacre, Nottingham NG10 5HU
Telephone. 0602 391772

FOREWORD

AN ANONYMOUS PHILOSPHER, (whether male or female is open to question), recently divided the inhabitants of this Planet into three distinct sexes - men, women and COPPERS! If this were the case, which Heaven forbid, many of my counterparts as wives of Police officers may doubtless have wondered into which generic classification we would fall. When need arises we are often taken for granted as first class substitutes, in greater or lesser emergencies, when our menfolk are otherwise engaged in the detection of crime, or other calls of duty.

In the 1920's and '30's, with plenty of manpower available, the men selected by the hierarchy for entry into the Police Force had to be rather special. Any young man who succeeded in passing the stiff entrance examination, a strict intelligence test, whose height was not less than 5 feet 8 inches, whose general appearance and deportment passed the scrutiny of those putting him to the test, and appeared to have all the attributes considered essential for the making of a first class Police Officer, considered himself fortunate indeed to have landed what was in those days known to be a rare fish — a good steady job with regular pay and opportunities for promotion, and above all a generous pension at the end of it all.

In light-hearted vein, I take a look into life as seen through my own eyes as the wife of a Police Sergeant serving during the '40's and early '50's. The book travels through the tense moments of my strict 'vetting' by a neutral member of the Force as to my suitability to become the wife of an officer of the Law, before being granted official permission to wed my man.

Many personal experiences are recalled through part of Hitler's World War 2 and five years of its aftermath to our eventual retirement to our country cottage with roses round the door, and the seemingly inevitable ten paces ....!

For obvious reasons I have refrained from disclosing any trade secrets, or causing distress to individuals mentioned in the book. It all happened in the East Midlands, but similar conditions and situations could have occurred almost anywhere.

Life in the '40's for the majority of ordinary folk was really very tough. Money was scarce, the authority of senior officials inside or outside the Force was never questioned, and discipline reigned supreme, with few exceptions, from cradle to grave. Until the outbreak of the war it was unusual for a married woman to need, or even desire, to find satisfaction by seeking employment outside her own home. In the case of police wives this was rather different. Our co-operation was taken for granted, and given generally unstintingly.

As custodians of a Police Station, albeit quite a small one, we, the Broughtons, found life frugal, sometimes frustrating, even a little alarming, but never inactive or boring, and our combined sense of humour often steered us through a sticky patch or delicate situation. When our war-scarred spirits were low, we could always dream of that lovely carrot dangling ahead — the pension which would regularly fall into our lap after twenty-five years, or more, of good and faithful service — assuming the male member of the partnership lived to stay the course!

DEDICATION

To John, my long-suffering Police Sergeant Husband, who kept carpet sweeper, dishmop and teapot on active service while I was otherwise engaged in bashing out this burst of nostalgia on my faithful old typewriter.

Wynne Broughton

Contents

Page

PART 1 : FIRST SENTENCE — 4 YEARS' HARD

1. Tealeaves Don't Lie — 1
2. Getting Down To It — 13
3. Bombs in Paradise — and Elsewhere — 27
4. Bobbies, Boozers and Bad Lads — 31
5. Pregnant Pause — and a Honeymoon for Three — 39
6. On The Move — 61

PART 2 : SECOND SENTENCE — 7 YEARS' HARD

7. Home is the Cop-Shop — Outside Privies and All — 67
8. All in the Day's Work — 79
9. H.P., A Ghost, and a Graveyard Safari — 97
10. Doggies, Moggies and Other Dumb Friends — 103
11. Pyorrhoea, Agoraphobia, and the Little White Pill — 109
12. Hail Peace — Farewell? Ten Paces...... — 119
13. Freedom Spells Country Cottage, and Oh No! Not Another 10-Pace Trip — 127

ELEVEN YEARS' HARD
(or TEN PACES TO THE PRIVY)

PART I : FIRST SENTENCE — 4 YEARS' HARD

CHAPTER 1

Tealeaves Don't Lie

'Win Killer, you're going to get entangled with the Law,' said Jane.
'What d'ya mean? Land in Court, end up in gaol? Heaven forbid,' was my immediate reply.
'No, silly, nothing as deadly as that.'
'Explain yourself at once. The suspense is killing me.'
'You're going to wed a Cop.'
'Don't be ridiculous. I don't even know any Coppers. I think they're better kept at arm's length,' I said with a finality I hoped would silence my second-sighted office colleague who was still pointing to the brown mass of tealeaves left in my cup, now drained of the pale tasteless liquid concoction officially known as the 3.15 tea-break brew, otherwise dubbed by most as cuckoo-wee, or worse.

Still aware of my apparent disbelief, and not to be put off she continued:-
'You can't get away from it as easily as that, because it's all here. Now it's no use trying to ignore it. Come on, pay attention and look. It's far more reliable than stargazing. Cast your eyes down to the bottom of the cup. There's his helmet, and those little twists must be his handcuffs, and that long one must be his truncheon.'

I shook my head visibly, not believing one word of her prognostication.
'All right then, if you're still not convinced, look at those two shapes above the rest, wedding bells they are, or my name's not Jane.'

I looked, shook my head in complete disbelief, and proceeded to transcribe the copious shorthand notes in my book on to the typewriter. The tealeaf tale was promptly forgotten.

That small incident, as unlikely as it was incredulous, took place during the midsummer of 1936. Now here I am, exactly four years later, at the almost too late age for marrying, according to the young members of the office staff, namely thirty-three years, a Copper's Bride of ten hours, all alone, a little weepy, and without Sergeant John Broughton by my side. What's even harder to bear is the fact that I am lying, propped up with two cushions, on the lounge floor behind the piano, pet budgie, Pete, in his cage at my feet, and our Fox Terrier pup fast asleep across my bosom. What a disastrous wedding night!

But where is your espoused, you may well ask. He must be an absolute cad to desert you so soon after taking his vows. Perhaps the day's excitement had proved too much for him and he had taken fright? Fortunately for both of us it was nothing like that.

All our wedding guests had departed. John and I were about to discard our wedding day regalia and begin the process of getting used to each other, when the very last thing we expected really happened.

The quiet stillness of that July night in the year 1940 was broken, completely shattered in fact, by the shrill 'oo-er-oo-er-oo' NOT-TONIGHT-YOU-DON'T threat of Ilkeston Town's main air raid warning siren, known otherwise as 'Moanin' Minnie' or MM for short. From her Co-op. shop rooftop vantage point, within a short stone's throw of John's Police Headquarters, she bellowed forth her clarion call, as she had done many times since our war against Hitler had begun some ten months earlier. The siren seemed to say:-

Take cover at once, You will if you're wise,
For you never can tell what may fall from the skies.

This advice was all very well for members of the general public. To every Copper, of whatever rank, and that included my John, it abruptly put paid to all leisure pursuits, even our enforced stay-at-home honeymoon. It meant GET OUT ON DUTY AS FAST AS YOU CAN.

'No use, I'll have to go', he said, meekly apologetic, yet resignedly, as he changed into his uniform. I received a hasty peck on the cheek as he tore himself away to the post of duty, with no time to dwell on the thought of what might have been.

'I should come downstairs, if I were you,' he called as he sped below.

I heard the rattle of his tin shrapnel-proof hat as he lifted it from the peg in the hall. The door closed behind him. I began to quake a little.

This was no time for nerves, and I consoled myself by thinking it was possibly a false alert such as we had experienced before — a kind of little wedding night joke played on us by Hitler and his satellites.

I almost leapt down the fourteen stairs into the hall, and wondered how John was faring, as he pedalled his way through the blacked out streets on his old two-wheel velocepede, alias that ageing rigid, rapid, reliable Raleigh bike, which had covered countless peacetime miles, and was destined to transport him still many more at least until hostilities ended.

I counted myself fortunate to be able to remain indoors while he would have to trudge the streets with the prospect of bombs coming in all directions.

Now 'Manorby' our very first home, kindly rented for us by the County Council, was the proud possessor of many of the mod-cons of that era. The one exception, typical of so many Police owned or rented properties at that time, was the toilet. In peacetime this healthily situated detached mini-building had been taken as inevitable by those who trotted to and from its portals by day or night. In these scarey days and nights of war torn Britain it was easy to envisage the inconvenience of this type of convenience.

Some lucky people can wait for hours, a whole day even, before spending a penny. I, alas, was never in that category. In fact, during times of stress or crisis, my waterworks are the first to respond adversely, when urgency is the keynote of relief. Tonight was no exception. GO I MUST, even if my goal is situated ten paces from the back door.

The burning question of the moment was, dare I risk taking those perilous steps into the great black unfamiliar in search of instant comfort, knowing the attendant risk of being struck by some flying missile from above?

Unwilling to 'christen' any of the kitchen utensils, with fingers (and legs) crossed, I sallied forth into the night, spent the quickest penny of my life, and returned to the refuge of home from my outside sit-on, with palpitating heart but happily unscathed.

I returned briefly to the bedroom, soliloquising as I mounted the stairs on the inhumanity of the German Race in general, and on Hitler and the current war in particular. Somewhat ruefully, I thought, 'Ah well, if the worst happens, I suppose they'll find me and pick up the pieces!'

'In any case,' I consoled myself, 'It's surely unlikely that the good Lord, or whoever is in charge, could be so cruel as to deny my new husband and me at least a few days, weeks, or months of married bliss. Or could He? What if He had listed all my past transgressions and shortcomings, and decided to end it all with a spot of bomb treatment before I did any more damage?'

'For Heaven's sake, Winifred Killer.... Oh dear, I've forgotten already I'm a Broughton now,' I said aloud — a habit of mine when in a tight corner, 'Think positive and organise yourself.'

Still fully clothed, I grabbed the nearest blanket from our brand new bed, collected my handbag containing, as usual, very little cash, a few personal documents and the usual incidentals to be found in any woman's hold-all. Quickly I ran downstairs in order to release the first of my male companions, our claustrophobic, disaster-sensing, howling, quivering pup, nicknamed Roger the Lodger. Next I unhooked Pete-the-Tweet's cage from its stand. It seems incredible but as I took hold of the cage, the night cover slipped to the floor, revealing a very wide awake little blue bird who, looking straight into his mirror which he was steadying with one of his claws, piped out his current pet phrase, taught to him by one of John's colleagues:-

'Bugger Hitler, bugger 'im, bugger 'im,' he repeated several times, followed by 'Wring his bloody neck, wring his bugger,....'

'Pete, old boy,' I admonished, 'If ever you fall into the hands of the enemy, and YOU say THAT, it won't be Hitler's neck that's wrung.'

It may have been misguided optimism, or the fact that John and I had been too busy in other directions, but in the rush of preparing our home, neither of us had made any preparations against a sudden onslaught by the enemy from the skies. Apart from blacking out all the windows and screening both back and front doors, nothing had been further from our minds than self protection inside against the foe without.

'Oh dear, where shall we dig in tonight?' I asked my two pets. A little whine from Roger and a tweet from Pete indicated that if ever I had a great chance to use my initiative it was right now.

There was a tiny under-stairs pantry which might have given good cover, but this was already full to capacity with various cases and boxes we had not had time to unpack. So as a safety zone that was unthinkable.

The Lounge? Just the thing I thought, for had not one of my friends mentioned recently that she adapted her's when necessary, using the piano as a kind of blast screen.

Now that Broadwood upright overstrung iron framed instrument of ours must have been quite the weightiest of all time. I struggled and tugged, I pulled and shoved, and eventually, short of giving myself a hernia, I gave up the effort, having just managed to move one end of it far enough from the wall to make room for my recumbent body and that of Roger — if he could be persuaded to settle there.

As I prepared our makeshift bed-cum-air-raid-shelter, I could not help comparing that small lump of quaking canine fur and flesh, now dithering apprehensively beside me, with his normal aggressive behaviour typical of his breed.

For three months before our wedding, he had shared John's lodgings in the Town, hence 'the lodger' handle to his name. From there to all four corners of the area our faithful friend had quickly gained the reputation as the fiend who tormented all the local pussycats. He it was who liked no sport better than to engage in combat with every dog, large, medium or small, he happened to meet. Lofty Alsation or tiny Peke he confronted with equal temerity and panache, sending them squealing for cover. Our four-legged bully-boy did not win every battle, however, for this young aggressor bore a permanently perforated ear and a three inch hairless leg scar as proof of at least two wars he definitely lost!

'A proper little 'Itler 'e is', said one of the neighbours, whose Ginger Tomcat had learned by experience to respect our belligerent pup.

Yet, at this moment, reflecting on my own present mood of nervous apprehension, I decided that abnormal times were doubtless responsible for the change in the behaviour patterns not only of human beings but of animals generally, and perhaps dogs in particular.

Our triangular hidey-hole now prepared, I arranged the cushions from the settee to form an improvised mattress on the floor, with two downier ones on which to lay my head.

I covered up Pete's cage once more, planted my bottom on the 'paliasse' and lay down with my head in the acute angle formed between wall and piano back. I swear my posterior bore the imprint of that ridged skirting board for weeks after the experience.

'Come on, Roger,' I said, gathering him in my arms. He lay uneasily at my side. I draped the blanket over us both. He placed his two front paws over my bosom. He breathed several deep doggie sighs, and before I could say 'night-night' he was away in canine dreamland.

As for me, I just could not manage to drop off. I tried everything I knew as sleep inducers, from counting sheep and numbers to repeating rhymes and the Lord's Prayer. All to no avail.

Before long I fell into a pleasant nostalgic reverie.

I recalled my first date with John, for which I turned up more than an hour late owing to pressure of work at the office. I arrived puffing and panting and full of apologies.

'Sorry I'm so disgustingly late' said breathless me, having run at least a mile at record speed, and not really expecting him to be still waiting in his car. 'You see the boss came in late and insisted on dictating several urgent letters, and, and.....'

'Now don't stand there apologising,' said my patient friend, 'Jump in and settle down', as he opened the car door. 'Where would you like to go. A drink somewhere perhaps?'

I grinned to myself thinking that as I worked at a Brewery he expected me to be pickled in alcoholic stimulants. 'I don't drink, at least nothing stronger than mineral waters. They didn't dub me 'Lemonade Lil' at the Office for nothing!'

We laughed. The ice was broken.

After a quick visit and short chat in the Snug of a country Pub we discovered a quiet spot in a leafy lane several miles from my home. It seemed a pity not to take advantage of the lovely bright evening, the sky romantically lit up by a brilliant full moon, sparklingly alive with myriads of twinkling stars. the night was still young, we were new to each other, and there seemed so much to discuss.

John, to whom I was introduced some twelve months after the tealeaf forecast, confessed his love of music, particularly the lighter Classics, on which I also had been schooled. Alas the piano at my home was neglected in recent years. Perhaps our mutual affection for things musical might change this state of affairs after all.

'As a matter of fact,' he told me, 'I do fiddle a bit.' And before I could say G-string, he jumped out of the car and from the back seat, produced a violin and bow from their case. I joined them on the grass verge.

'Play on, Yehudi 2,' I said, wondering what kind of a maestro, or otherwise, he was.

'How about this for starters?' he asked, as the strains of Dvorak's Humoresque pervaded the stillness of the night air.

Unexpectedly as it was sudden, the whole countryside began bursting into life. The hooting of an owl perched in a tall hedge close by began it all. He was quickly joined by the urgent flapping of wings and tweet-tweetings of all kinds of feathered friends from their treetop perches. Then came some warm, friendly cooings of several local wood pigeons, anxious to play their part in augmenting the strange new sound in their usually tranquil lane.

Several classical snatches later I noticed two bright round orbs, torchlike and irridescent, shining in our direction. As they grew closer, we saw they were attached to the head of a very large plump cow, or maybe it was a bull, who moo-ed her, (or his), warm deep basso profundo encore — or perhaps it was a boo of disapproval. We shall never know, but it did succeed in adding a velvety touch to the carnival of animals and birds.

Not to be outdone, a flock of sheep in an adjoining field bleated loudly as they advanced in formation, inquisitive no doubt as to where all the fuss was taking place.

As my fiddling wizard changed his tune for the nth time, two huge carthorses came galloping across the field, whinneying madly as they clippety-clopped towards us, tails flying in the air.

'nero? yehudi? no - just JB serenading WK'

'Watch out,' was my anxious plea to John, 'They're going to jump the gate. If they do it's God help us.'

'And the car,' he added.

As we bolted into the road, a safe distance in case the worst happened, both horses stopped dead, inches short of their side of the gate.

'I think it's time we moved on, don't you, or we might be confronted with an irate farmer with shotgun,' said John.

The Stradivarius??? was duly put to bed. Peace reigned once more, and after chatting for a few minutes, John asked if I would meet him again some time.

We both felt that, impromptu and charming as it was unique, that unrehearsed symphony of animals, birds, beasts and humans would be an ever-living memory. Strange, but until that evening I had never associated policemen with an appreciation of music, least of all GOOD MUSIC.

Further meetings followed as and when John's somewhat awkward split duty times of mainly four hours on and four hours off, allowed. I did not fail to notice that the Big-Wigs in the Force, alias the hierarchy, in our County at least, who arranged the duty sessions of the lesser mortals, must possess an anti-social, sadistic sense towards them.

For two years we managed to meet at least once weekly on his off duty day......

Oh dear, I do feel so weary, but somehow sleep is as far away as ever. It's bad enough to be deserted by a brand new husband, but when sleep refuses to come, it makes the night so long.

I shone the torch towards the clock. 12.15 and still no sign of his return.

I'll try my left side and see what happens. Nothing did, except my thoughts continued to stray over the past.

Where was I? Oh yes. I'll never forget the day I announced our engagement to the Boss.

It was in the Spring of 1939. John and I spend a weekend in Blackpool. No, it wasn't one of THOSE weekends. It was all strictly two single rooms and no hanky-panky either, which in those days was the rule. On our first evening there, after dinner, we strolled round the shops. We stopped outside a brilliantly lit jeweller's shop.

'See anything you fancy,' asked John, as we scanned the ring window.

'That's a beauty over there,' said I, pointing to a big saphhire ringed with diamonds at £450, 'isn't it.'

'If you'll lower your standards rather more than a little, I might treat you,' he laughed.

'Engagement?' I queried, having felt this was imminent.

'Why not? We'll never get a better chance.'

And, before I could say 'This is so sudden' we were inside the shop, JB insisting that his limit of £20 was dead earnest.

We selected a three diamond ring at £18.50, and left the shop.

Less than twenty paces away the ring was unceremoniously placed on the appropriate finger of my left hand.

'I guess my family will think we should have waited a little while longer, especially as it looks as if war with Hitler's lot will be declared any time now.' I said.

'Good Heavens, my girl,' he told me, 'The war, if it comes, will probably last for years, and neither of us is very young, are we?'

'Don't rub it in,' I remonstrated.

We returned home. The next hurdle was to tell the family of our plans. No objection was anticipated or raised. Telling the Boss, however, could be quite a problem.

I arrived at the office early, in good time for combat. HCO, as we knew the boss, abhorred any changes in his staff, and had a very poor view of the married status anyway.

Following the usual hour or so of staff torment, I seized the opportunity to throw down the gauntlet, so to speak. His reply much of which will not bear repetition, included:-

'You bloody fool, you blasted little idiot. You must be stark staring mad to think of leaving a comfortable well paid job like yours to marry a bloody struggling Copper. Why, on his screw, he won't be able to keep you in knickers and nightgowns. Now look here, I'm determined to knock some sense into your bloody thick ear.'

I felt nothing short of a spot of silent diplomacy was required at this stage, so let him rant on.

'I'll tell you here and now, I've had a bloody-nuff of women in the office. I'm abso-bloody-lutely fed up with the lot of you. You're all the blasted same, always hankering after getting wed. One day, and I mean this, I'll sack the bloody lot of you and have some sensible men instead. They're thankful to stay with me. It's pretty obvious to me you've no idea what you're letting yourself in for. I've not been friendly with at least three Chief Constables not to know a great deal about the workings of the underlings in the Force.

'You'll probably be shipped off to some outlandish village, have to exist in an antiquated, cold, cheerless stone-built cottage in the frozen north of the County. You'll have no bathroom, and it'll be a day's march to the 'bog' at the bottom of the garden. There, on a winter's night, you'll sit and freeze, probably get icicles on your rear, or catch pneumonia, as the wind whistles through the ill-fitting door and up through the hole in the side of the wall where stands the old tin pan catcher in all its stinking glory.

'Your night's sleep will be regularly disturbed by the clippety-clopping of old 'Flannel Foot' alias the maramalade cart, as at dead of night it advances slowly, stopping at each cottage to collect what is generally called shit, more politely known by the 'refained' folk as 'night soil'. I'm right, you know. There's more Coppers' houses with outside privies than inside.'

'But.....' I tried to put a stop to his forebodings, without success.

'Don't you But me,' he retorted. 'I've not done with you yet. You don't seem to realise you'll be at the beck and call of everyone from the Chief Constable to the youngest poor devil on the beat, and from the local Squire to the tiniest Tot of a kid who happens to fall in the 'Cut'.'

'You'll be tied to the telephone all day and all night, when your dearly beloved Copper is out tracking down everyone from murderer to cattle rustler. You'll have drunks and all kinds of louts forever at your door. In other words you'll be doing penal servitude for the rest of his service, and you won't get one penny for your part of the bargain. People will ostracise you, and social life will be non-existent. The only friends you'll make will be the wives of other Cops, who'll be as bloody bored as you are, and all jealously looking forward to the promotion of their spouses, which'll never come!'

'Will that be all?' I enquired as he appeared to have run out of steam.

'Just you think about it. Break it off before you get too involved.'

'I'd prefer to forget it. In any case the wedding will not be taking place for some months, perhaps a year hence.'

Little did I realise that on this very day, DUTY would tear my husband away for heaven knows how long. At least a tiny part of HCO's predictions contained a tiny spot of truth!

All that is past history. Why did my uneasy mind have to recall such unlikely forebodings? Wish I could just lose myself if only for a few hours.

Still my weary thoughts strayed into the past. How fortunate I had been to pass the strict 'vetting' in order to be granted permission to marry a police officer.

After John had sent in his application to marry, I was interviewed by one of the local Police Officers. His interrogation was extremely thorough. His queries ranged from 'Do you get on well at home?' to 'What employment did your Grandfather and Father do?' Not fortgetting 'Have you ever committed a crime, trivial or worse', and 'Can you cook?'

I hastened to assure him that, apart from an occasional verbal scrap at home, we were a peace loving lot; that I had had no brushes with the Law, and so far as I could recollect, there were no skeletons in our cupboards. I had never been in debt, though more often skint than flush.

As regards my religious beliefs, in which he was also deeply interested, I informed him I could safely term mine as being those of a 'loose' Anglican (in the nicest sense). In other words, I had been raised in that faith, had attended Sunday School as a child and later taught the youngsters, but seldom attended Church at that time.

I assured him that my parents and forbears, or their relations, close or more distant, had never been in trouble with the Law, that my Grandfather, a farmer, was never guilty of sheep stealing or cattle rustling, and that bigamy had never formed part of any of our, or their, marital relations.

To avoid delving too deeply into the past so far as my own Mother's broken marriage was concerned, in reply to his searching questions regarding my Father, I was guilty on the spur of the moment of telling what I considered to be a tiny white lie, which succeeded in haunting me for some years to come. This, I must admit, was not simply because of the lie, but in case the Police authority should ever find me out and boot me out of the Force!

'My Father has passed on,' I told my inquisitor, as delicately as I could muster, accompanying my lying statement with the saddest look I could put on my face.

'I'm so very sorry,' he replied with feeling.

And thank goodness he left it at that.

I should explain that in the strict sense of that phrase describing my Dad's departure this was quite untrue. Yet more than twenty years earlier he had *passed out* of our lives, having deserted the obviously love-less nest, leaving my Mum and six chicks to face the world alone, practically penniless and with no clue as to his whereabouts.

Ironically, some years later we did hear of his demise in the South of England. If the family name in the telephone directory had been Smith instead of KILLER, my lie might still have been on my conscience.

Permission to marry came through shortly afterwards, together with the information that we could take up residence in Manorby, the little semi-detached house with which we had fallen in love several weeks previously.

Another glance at the clock. Oh dear, it's only 2.25, and still no sign of John. What a day it has been. Wish I could get off to sleep.

I'm oh so weary. As a wedding day it had been more of a NO day in most respects.

NO FESTIVE BELLS. NO BRIDAL GOWN. NO NUPTIAL FEAST. NO HONEYMOON. NO LOVING.

We had already accepted all the means of self denial expected of us all in these days of war, even on what is traditionally reputed to be the greatest day in the life of any girl who ever went a'courtin'.

Adolf Hitler and his satellites, who just ten months earlier had left no option to our Country and France but to declare war on him, pitchforking us into all the horrors and stringencies of war, was entirely to blame for universal economies.

Make-do-and-mend, Never-buy-two-if-one-will-do, were two of the many slogans uppermost in our minds. Smearing our toast with the thinnest scraping of insipid margarine had constituted the national breakfast routine, and butter-laced crumpets for tea were just a mouth-watering memory.

Shortages were already spurring on the busy housewife to perform amazing feats of ingenuity in the kitchen, and petrol rationing had reduced private motoring and public transport to a minimum.

Who were we therefore not to conform? After all, our own wedding day sacrifices were insignificant when weighed against the privations of countless others more directly involved in the conflict, both at home and overseas.

NO BELLS? The ringing of all Church bells was forbidden by law for the duration of the war. They were to be rung only in the event of invasion of our shores by the enemy. Thus, no Grandsire triples or Treble Bob Minors greeted our wedding party on arrival or departure at the Church.

NO FEAST? At this stage in the war food was becoming very scarce. Sugar, fats and meat had been rationed since March, so a super wedding spread by way of a large reception had not even been contemplated. In any case, travel by public or private transport was so unpredictable that we had no idea how many guests would be able to make the journey. Our buffet 'Do' at Manorby, though frugal, with the help of many resourceful home cooks, had proved a huge success.

NO BRIDAL GOWN? In my teens I had always dreamed, as most young girls do, of a voluminous white silken dress with long train and frothy veil, a diamond tiara to top it all. To spend my hard-earned limited savings on a complete bridal outfit, which could not possibly be re-created into something useful for later wear would, I knew, have been an unnecessary extravagance. Instead I settled for a modest two-piece suit in Nottingham Lace of a delicate strawberry shade, costing a mere four guineas (£4.20).

NO HONEYMOON? All police leave had been cancelled. The County boundaries were the limit of our travels. What better than a cosy little 'get together' in our own new home surroundings?

NO LOVING? None so far. I wonder when that errant husband of mine will be released from duty.

Suddenly my reverie was shattered. Roger leapt from my side barking furiously. Bang, rattle, bang on the front door sent me hot all over. Had something awful happened to John? The only way to find out was to answer the urgent call.

Expecting bad news, I cautiously opened the door just a chink. To my utter relief there stood John, bright and cheerful in contrast to my still sleepy countenance.

'Sorry to disturb you,' he hastened to tell me, 'But in the hurry and flurry of excitement last night I quite forgot to take my key.

By then it was broad daylight, and a glance at the clock told me it was 7.45 a.m. I must have fallen asleep after all during my nostalgic session.

'Has the ALL CLEAR gone yet?' I enquired, having heard neither guns, planes nor sirens since bedding down.

'Oh yes,' he replied, 'About two hours ago. I'm sure you'll be relieved to know there was no enemy activity round here. But I had a few things to clear up at the office so stayed on for a while. Now I'm free all day, no more duty until 9 tomorrow night.'

'Night duty? Oh Gawd, your lot aren't half a sadistic gang of killjoys.' was my disappointed retort.

'You'll get used to this sort of carry on,' he tried to reassure me.

'I wonder.' Perhaps HCO had a point after all.

'By the way, how did you manage after I left last night?' he asked.

I showed him my improvised shake-down and described briefly how I had coped with the situation in our boudoir-shelter.

Having complimented me on my ingenuity, we shared a leisurely pot of tea, consigned Roger to his basket, Pete to his rightful hook, and together, according to the lyric, we 'climbed the wooden hill to Bedfordshire'.

As we prepared to resume where we had been so cruelly interrupted some ten hours previously, I recalled a highly appropriate Toast which had been recited by an extrovert member of my office staff at my farewell party:-

> Two little pillows trimmed with lace,
> Two little faces face to face,
> Everything else in its proper place —
> Here's hoping!

We both popped into bed.

'We shall remember yesterday as the non-event of our lives,' I quipped.

'What's wrong with today?'

'Nothing — so far.'

And so, for the present at least, we forgot the great big troubled world outside, heavily engaged in all the ravages of war, in favour of our own new, private little world inside our very first home.

'God bless those truthful tealeaves!'

CHAPTER 2
Getting Down To It

We rose just before noon. John took Roger for a stroll before we ate.

'What's for breakfast,' asked John on his return.

'Breakfast? It's more like lunch now. But first of all let's live it up with a glass of HCO's generous wedding gift Bubbly. How about a final Ritzy fling before we get down to our bread-and-butter (sorry margarine) life ahead?'

The meal over, while I dealt with the kitchen sink end of things, John went round to his former 'digs' to collect his uniform and various items he had not yet transferred.

Oh my goodness, THAT UNIFORM. There were simply stacks of it. Several suits to cover summer, winter, everyday and best wear, a massive great coat, two voluminous capes, masses of blue shirts, boots and leggings and an extra helmet, and this did not include his civilian clothes.

'Where on earth shall we store all that clobber?' I enquired.

'In the big wardrobe, so I'm afraid you'll have to put all your stuff in the one in the spare bedroom.'

'Charming. My STUFF indeed, already relegated to second class gear.'

Still it was no use making a fuss, but in view of all the recent events I was just beginning to realise that police duty and all its appendages would have to take precedence over all else, whether I liked it or not, in order to satisfy the hierarchy in the Constabulary and to keep the peace at home.

'Why on earth do they still make you wear those old fashioned capes?' I asked as he was busily stowing them away.

'They're really marvellous,' he assured me. 'For one thing they're so easy to put on and remove, they keep shoulders dry and warm without any bulky sleeves. And, although we don't broadcast it, the cape makes a perfect cover up within its folds for any innocent little gifts which may occasionally fall into the hands of the Law.'

'You don't mean to tell me you accept bribes, do you?' I asked somewhat apprehensively.

'Oh no, nothing of great value,' was his quick reply to allay my obvious fears, 'Sometimes an opportune call at one of the local Bakeries, to ensure all is well, will get a quick response from those in charge, that is, a small but harmless share of something just taken from the ovens. So you see, Win, nobody asks any questions on the way to the Office, and on arrival there, the gift is deposited in a convenient hiding place, although everyone there knows that the lovely home-bake type aroma pervading the air is definitely not the result of a visit to the Gas Works.'

'So long as there's no risk attached, then it's alright, I suppose.'

'Of course it's O.K. Anyway, better mortals than I in the Force are unofficially guilty of similar 'misdemeanours'. In any case, a harmless loaf of bread, a couple of sausage rolls, a link of black pudding or polony, or a few peppermints, could not really be construed by even the most fastidious law abiding member of the public or of the Force as anything but a kindly gesture to an ever-hungry copper! I know how far to go, don't worry.'

Secretly hoping he did, there could be no reply to that.

Kitchen chores, completed and, following a quick flick round with my feather duster, I decided to try to find a more or less permanent place for everything.

John, whose first wife had died four years ago, already had the basic suites of furniture found in most homes of that era. Thus we had been spared the expense of starting up home from scratch. Nevertheless there were various items I had collected prior to our wedding for which resting places had to be found. These included:-

Wooden Ironing Board which cost	1.11	(10p approx.)
Electric Iron	4.11	(25p approx.)
Set of 3 Aluminium Saucepans	9. 6	(48p approx.)
21-pice China Teaset	8. 6	(43p approx.)
1 pair Wool Blankets	1.15. 0	(£1.75 approx.)
2 pairs Cotton Sheets	2. 0. 0	(£2.00 approx.)
4 Pillowcases	4. 0	(20p approx.)
2 Bolster Cases	3.11	(20p approx.)
Zinc Bucket	6	(2.5p approx.)
Kitchen Scales	2.11	(15p approx.)
3 Mixing Bowls	3. 0	(15p approx.)
Secondhand Gas Boiler	1. 0. 0	(£1.00 approx.)
2 Wooden Deck Chairs	5. 0	(25p approx.)
Old Dewdrop (Jeremiah)	6	(2.5p approx.)

Old Dewdrop? Let me explain. This is a chamber pot, a guzunder, member mug or just plain po, according to the company you keep. You may think those things were on their way out, and you are correct. But I didn't buy it to USE. I fell for its decor. In view, however, of the gloomy forecasts of Mr. HCO, perhaps my sixpenny purchase might prove to the doubly useful.

Some six months before our wedding date I was walking round a country market, minding my own business, and ever mindful of the urgent need to avoid riotous spending. However, I could not allay my natural sense of curiosity when I espied a large crowd of people some ten or twelve deep, at a pottery stall. Every few seconds there was a burst of raucous laughter coming from that large and attentive audience.

Still unable to let a real bargain pass me by, I joined the merry throng. There, standing on a beer crate dais, was the saleswoman, whom I had already heard was quite famous locally for her down to earth repartee when trying to flog some of her more personal items of merchandise. This was to prove no exception.

Holding the object of amusement by its handle, she described in the most picturesque language, this absolute necessity in every household from Buckingham Palace downwards. To my eyes it certainly was an object of scenic beauty, and the saleslady's humour was matched only by the work of the artist who had decorated both interior and exterior of the vessel, in exquisite taste.

Holding it up towards the sun, to prove it was fashioned in the finest of white china, she pointed out that for the right-handed handlers, on the nearside, was a highly coloured picture of Niagara Falls. For the left-handed, a similar reproduction, also in glorious technicolour, of Victoria Falls. Between the two, equally colourful, no doubt to prove there was no international bias, was a view of Lake Como.

It was, however, to the interior decor, with her various lewd quips, she drew most attention. No doubt, with tongue in cheek, the artist had painted on the bottom of the bowl, a larger than life pair of human eyes, one in the act of winking.

'All this for a modest tanner' she cried. 'Take it home, and you can prove to your friends you've had a pee beside the Falls.'

'What's a tanner compared with such unusual beauty,' I thought, as I produced my sixpence and passed it over the heads of the crowd. In exchange she handed the article to me, without any fuss — or wrapping. I walked quickly away, hoping no-one would recognise me, my latest objet d'art tucked under my arm.

After due consideration, and more rude remarks, from my family, it was dubbed 'Old Dewdrop'. Perhaps one day I'll grow daffodils in it.

Referring to the list of things I had now placed in their respective places, you may notice there is no mention of a FRYING PAN. The absence of this implement was deliberate. Normally this would have been placed at the top of my list. But long before we wed, John had told me his reasons for boycotting this instrument of torture. Torture? Yes, death even. How come?

Some years earlier, when attending a Lecture given by the then Home Office Pathologist, the late Professor Webster, his anti-frying pan advice was taken almost as law by his audience. In emphasizing to every member of the Police Force the importance of doing everything in their power to keep in the best of health, by means of exercise, good living, and above all, consuming sensible well cooked food, the Professor had warned:-

'Tell your wives to boycott the FRYING PAN. This invention of the devil has been responsible for the illnesses, deaths even, of more Coppers than the criminal himself.'

And, to ensure his message was being taken seriously, he added:-
'Oh yes, I don't deny it's quick and easy cooking, but the greasy, often half-cooked food it presents can lead only to chronic indigestion at best, or at worst, ulcers and the final curtain call.

So you see, who was I to flout this wise man's words of warning?

It seemed particularly apt, at this time during the war, that an anti-frying pan jingle, issued by the Ministry of Food, pinpointed the same argument:-

> When over-tired and worried,
> One gets the stomach-ache,
> A simple cure is NOT TO FRY,
> But BOIL, or STEAM, or BAKE.

Reverting to that famous gentleman for a brief moment, he gave a further bit of advice, not perhaps too relevant here, but worthy of repetition, if only as an excellent maxim for everybody generally, and to us in particular, as an important pointer to good health and well being.

'Take a regular daily visit to the toilet, loo or bog, even if it is halfway down the garden on an ice cold day. If necessary, arm yourself with a good book, newspaper, or magazine — Crossword puzzles are first-class constipation curers. Don't hurry things, then sure enough your visit will not be fruitless.'

Fruitless? Ah well, a rose by any other name.....

The Professor did not forget the fruit either.

'Eat an apple or some other fresh fruit every day,' he advised.

Most of the afternoon was spent in organising myself and everything else. After tea we both sat down to hear the latest news on the wireless and, we were fortunate to hear several lovely musical programmes.

We both rose early the following morning. The sun was shining brilliantly, and I decided to equip myself with our one and only shopping basket and take a safari to the local shops.

Less than fifty paces from home I came face to face with a woman of about my own age, who smiled pleasantly as she stopped to speak to me.

'Excuse me, but are you the new police wife from up the road?' she enquired.

'Yes, I am', I confessed, thinking that news must travel fast in this neck of the woods.

'I'm Mary, wife of that furnisher over there,' said she, pointing to a large shop whose windows were filled with all kinds of household requisites from wardrobes to whatnots.

'I'm Win, and my husband is one of the three Police Sergeants stationed here. I'm a stranger, having come from nine miles away, but it should not take me long to settle down.'

I told her of my experience during the air raid alert, and she apologised for laughing when I described my unique hidey-hole.

'We have a very good strong air raid shelter at the rear of the shop, which we share with several people living nearby. Now promise me you will come and join us any time you hear the siren, won't you,' she said, and really appeared to mean it.

At that moment I could have picked up and hugged that dear lady from sheer relief at the prospect of no more solo performances during the hours of peril. In fact, so delighted was I that I almost looked forward to the next clarion call of Moanin' Minnie.

She showed me round the shelter and invited me to her house for coffee and a chat.

I mentioned that I was on my way to see the shops and to register our names for groceries and meat rations.

'I should go to Steak-an'-Kid Sid for meat, if I were you. You won't get any extra from him, but he has good stuff and is very fair. His shop's almost opposite ours.'

'Thanks for the tip, I will.'

'You'll need a grocer too, won't you?'

'Please enlighten me on all your usual shops, and I'll gradually introduce myself.'

'Well, there's Floury Fred, who dishes out all kinds of groceries, just up the road from Sid's. Tell him I sent you. He's pretty good when any scarcities are temporarily relieved.'

'Do you have nicknames for all your traders?' I asked, somewhat intrigued by Sid and Fred's.

'There are several more. How about Whalemeat Wally, who sells various types of fish when available. You usually have to queue outside his shop which he only opens those days when he's lucky enough to receive his small quota. He used to sell rabbits too, but they're almost non-existent now. They're not counted as rationed meat, you see. Doughnut Doll is an amusing character. She sells bread and a few cakes. She'll tell you she never eats her sweet things as she's suffered from violent indigestion for twenty years! Fruit & Veg. Reg is worth a call. He usually has good fresh vegetables, and he'll lose no time in telling you about his operation, and his wife will interrupt his story by telling you about her sister who died in childbirth.'

'All very enlightening. Are there others you have dubbed similarly?'

'Oh yes, I almost forgot Fry Tonight Flo. She makes excellent chips, that is when her fat ration arrives. Fifty-Bob Bert might be useful to you if ever you can save up enough clothing coupons for one of his suits. I mustn't forget HMD the Registrar, you may need him if you have any family. He's the Hatch, Match and Despatch specialist. You've already met Trev. the Rev., who must have married you.'

'What a lovely list. I might be able to think of a few more myself when I've settled down,' was my laughing response to her list.

'You might be amused to know they've dubbed my Husband Spring Heeled Jack. I understand it's no misnomer, because he's seldom still!'

I left Mary still laughing, and proceeded to call on Sid.

On entering the shop I at once came face to face with a small, Tweedledum like figure of a man, obviously a fine advertisement for his trade — raised no doubt on prime cuts of beef.

I introduced myself, and registered with him for our twice-times 1/10d. (9p x 2) worth of weekly meat. As I was about to leave the shop, I asked if he could let me have a supply of bones with my usual rations.

'Bones?' he queried. 'I didn't think you modern housewives bothered about 'em these days.'

'Ah, but I was raised on bone broth - the backbone of the nation, my Mother used to say, hence my faith in them. With plenty of added veg. they make wonderful fillers. We often enjoyed her bone stew before I left home, and they'll eke out my rations here, I am sure.'

'It shall be done, my dear.'

Next I visited Fred, whose shop smelt temptingly inviting — an unforgettable aroma of cheese, bacon, spices and other items displayed on the shelves.

He promised to look after me for my 12ozs. of sugar, half pound of fats, 2 ozs. of tea (twice) each week.

'Anything else that comes along, you'll be welcome to share with our other regulars,' he said reassuringly.

From then on that kindly man and his staff proved to be so utterly generous, not by giving me extra rations which, as the wife of a Police Officer I would have been bound to refuse, but whenever a scarce commodity came to hand, sometimes 'under the counter', sometimes openly, he always ensured that it was surreptitiously placed among my other purchases with never a spoken word. There were times when I felt I could hardly afford the extras that he bestowed on me, perhaps a few prunes, some dried fruit, a jelly, a tin of syrup even, or some other hard to come by item. Yet I dared not refuse them in case of giving offence, or for fear the supply might dry up altogether.

A couple of days later, I received a 'phone message from the Office, known by the serving Officers as THE TOP, asking me to call on Steak-an'Kid-Sid with the request that he should visit the Office at his early convenience.

I dashed over to his shop, arriving well before opening time. I knocked on the back door, which was opened by his wife.

'I have a message from THE TOP,' I told her, 'For your Husband.'

'Oh yes, do come in,' she said invitingly, 'He's just having his breakfast. Go through.'

I did as instructed and arrived in the kitchen, a small neat homely place.

As I entered, I could not help noticing that Sid was tucking heartily into the biggest fillet steak I had seen since the outbreak of war. That gentleman was quick to notice the glint of surprise, or I should say envy, in my eyes, as he cut another sliver from his massive, bloody oozing steak.

'Well now, Missus, YOU wouldn't eat MARG. if you were a GROCER, would you?'

'I never said a word,' I laughed. 'You must be a thought reader.'

'I'm glad I'm a butcher,' he grinned, 'Especially at breakfast time!'

I duly delivered the message, as he soaked up the reminder of the steak juice with a piece of bread.

'Aye, I'll go up shortly.'

So saying, he disappeared into the shop, murmuring as he went:-

'Don't go yet. Stop and have a word with the wife.'

As we were talking, Sid reappeared carrying a small package, saying:-

'Here you are, take this home with you. I hope you'll find it to your liking. Thanks for the message.'

'It's very kind of you,' I said, hoping there might possibly be a tasty morsel hidden within its wrapping.

'Now, dearie,' he said, 'There's no law, even in wartime, against me giving you a little welcoming present, is there? But keep it under your hat. Sarge and I have always got on well together, but this is the first time I've given him anything.'

Thinking 'I hope it won't be the last', I said aloud, 'Can't think of such a law, but then I'm not a Copper.'

I left Sid, and hurried home. I opened the little parcel, and there before my very eyes were two steaks, bigger even than the one old Sid had been gorging.

The memory of those scrumptious undercuts still lingers. In fact, no others even since the end of the war have ever tasted quite so good.

One week later, MM repeated her clarion call to take cover, warning us once more that Hitler's bomb-bearing birds, with hate in their hearts and destruction on their minds, were on their way to drop their dastardly visiting cards.

It was just before 9 in the evening. John whisked off on his bike. I bedded down Roger and Pete and, fully prepared for operation quick dash over the road, I hastened along to Mary's refuge. There certainly was some enemy activity somewhere as the sound of distant guns was heard. After less than an hour the All Clear sounded, and all eleven of us scampered home feeling nothing but relief that at least this time we had escaped from inherent danger.

Mary and I knew instinctively that we were kindred spirits. I was indeed grateful to have found a pal with whom I could chat, discuss the latest news, cooking triumphs and problems, the latter of which I had quite a few, and generally feel at home.

During the second week of our No-Honeymoon-John-working-by-night period, Mary asked me over for a cup of tea.

I arrived, feeling and no doubt looking, somewhat flushed and frustrated.

'Anything wrong?' queried Mary, 'You're looking rather tired.'

'Everything', I replied disconsolately.

'Oh dear, that doesn't sound like a very good start for married life. You're not regretting taking the plunge already, are you?'

'No, it's not that, but it's not funny either.'

'Go on, then, tell me all about it, let me be your Mother confessor. You know what they say about a trouble shared,' she quipped.

'Now, let me see,' I pondered, 'Which will you have first — the bread or the cake?'

'Figuratively or literally?' she asked.

'It has to be literally, oh woe is me, alas and alack.'

'Well, my Mum always said bread before cake,' said Mary, 'So let's have it that way round, shall we?'

'Here goes then. I got up extra early this morning, intending to make the most delicious batch of bread we'd ever tasted. I would have brought you a sample, but when I tell you its history, from the dough-ey stage, I thought you might not fancy it. If ever I have another go and it's palatable and presentable, I'll bring you some.'

'Oh dear, sounds ominous, but carry on. I'm all ears.' she encouraged.

'I began, as Mother did, with a big well in the centre of the bowl of flour and salt, added the yeast and water mixture, taking care not to 'drown the miller'. (In case you haven't heard this before, it means adding too much water when you've run out of flour). Having mixed and kneaded the sticky mass until it looked more or less like the old family dough had done, I placed bowl and contents in the dining room hearth, hoping the warmth from the fire would help the rising process.

'As I returned from my bent to erect position, my head inadvertently touched the stem of John's pipe overhanging the mantelpiece. Of course it was well filled with half smoked baccy. Down came a shower of ash, spreading all over the top of my beloved mix before I had time to cover up the contents of the bowl with a cloth.'

'Did you blow it off?' asked Mary.

'I did try, in fact I huffed and puffed with great vigour in an attempt to remove the offending foreign bodies, but that myriad of tiny specks stuck like glue.'

'So you left it in the hope it would not show up too much when baked?' asked Mary.

'Not likely. My first impulse was to throw the lot away, and keep the disaster secret. But WASTE NOT, WANT NOT rang in my ears. No, my dear, I persevered. With knife, spoon and more heavy breathing, I managed to remove most of it, hoping the end product would be edible.'

'Well then, what are worrying about?' asked Mary.

'That's only the beginning of its adventures. I left the rising function to progress while I set about doing a few household chores. I was dusting down the stairs when I noticed the absence of my signet ring, worn for many years on the little finger of my right hand. It had always been slightly loose but had never actually dropped off.'

'Now don't tell me it was dough-bound,' said Mary.

'You're dead right, it was, but finding it meant a thorough search into the doughey depths. My search for gold proved fruitless, and I consoled myself that it must have come off some other time.'

'I can't see why you are worrying so much,' said Mary.

'You would have if you'd been in my shoes. I flattened out the dough and left it to do its best, or worst. The 'phone rang. I answered it. A wrong number. I returned to the 'bakery', and there to my utter chagrin was our lively young pup, standing on his hind legs, front paws inside the bowl, whisker and eyebrow deep in my accident-prone bread to be.'

'No, not exactly, he was just enjoying himself wallowing in his new found edible mass, egged on no doubt by Pete the Tweet saying 'Who's a good boy then?'

'I think I'd have given up at that stage,' said Mary with feeling.

'No, I always enjoy a challenge, even if it hurts. In any case yeast and flour are in short supply these days. So, for better or worse, I tinned it, proved it, placed all four loaves in the oven, and hoped my blessing would counteract its curses.'

'I bet it will be scrumptious,' said Mary.

'We'll have to eat it now, and I've decided not to say anything about it to John until the last slice has been consumed.'

'What a morning you've had, Win.'

'My second name must be calamity Jane, I think. My culinary prowess took yet another turn for the worse when I decided to make a coconut cake while the oven was still hot after the bread came out. I swear that when cooked it weighed heavier than when it went into the cooker. It felt like a bomb.'

'Did you over-coconut it,' she asked. 'Is it a dead loss?'

'Not so far. I'll try out the first wedge on John for tea today. If he dies of indigestion, I'll consign it to the bin. Now I must dash, and prepare to serve up home-baked speckled bread and heavy cake to John.'

'Let me know his reaction,' said Mary, as I sped away.

Mary and I met again the following day.

'I kept thinking about you at teatime yesterday,' said Mary, 'And wondering how you were faring.'

'We ate slice after slice of that carbohydrate-gold tipped concoction I called bread. I turned down the cake for obvious reasons. John begged me to continue home baking, even after I told him we'd both get fat and podgy. And what do you think, the ring turned up half way down the first loaf. Fortunately I was cutting it so he was none the wiser!'

'Come in for a coffee,' said Mary, 'and I'll show you round our rambling old place.'

I did not need a second bidding.

On my first visit to her house I had noticed various items of newsprint adorning the walls of her kitchen. On entering this morning, I took a closer peek at them.

'I like your novel wallpaper,' I remarked as I read the cutting nearest to the door:-

>Reflect, whenever you indulge,
>It is not beautiful to bulge.
>A large untidy corporation
>Is far from helpful to the Nation!

'That's a bit of good advice,' said I with feeling, for I could always put on weight all too easily, but taking it off was the most difficult part.

Another one read:-

The crews of our minesweepers are always risking their lives to bring us food. DON'T WASTE ANY.

Our Dockers don't mind risking their lives to unload your food, but if you waste it their language is 'orrible.

Many slogans and other advice were put out by the radio, newspapers and posters, and these had not gone unnoticed by Mary and her scissors:-

Potato Pete, a drawing of a spud with face in various papers appeared regularly with some kind of recipe or other:-

> Said Mrs. A to Mrs. B
> Your meals have such variety,
> In vain for new ideas I hunt,
> I can't think how you do it.
>
> Said Mrs. B to Mrs. A
> At 8.15 a.m. each day
> I listen to THE KITCHEN FRONT,
> And after that GO TO IT!

Nearby were several more, including:-

> Eat the foods that give protection,
> And you need not fear infection,
> But can mix on equal terms
> With the most outrageous germs.

This one I found amusing:-

> I used to think one didn't oughter
> Make a soup with cabbage water!

This was a new one on me:-

> A daily cup of nettle tea
> Will keep the bile at bay you see.

The use of herbs featured in several jingles:-

> Now is the THYME to plant your herbs,
> SAGE folk know they'll be worth a MINT of money.

And

> P's for Protection potatoes afford,
> O's for the ounces of energy stored,
> T's for tasty and vitamins rich in
> A's for the art to be learnt in the kitchen,
> T's for the transport we need not demand,
> O's for Old England's own food from the land,
> E's for the energy eaten by you,
> S's for the spuds which will carry us through.

'It does occur to me,' I mentioned to Mary, 'That you are rather ruining your kitchen walls with this novel type of decor.'

'I don't mind one little bit,' was her reply. 'I'm determined to keep adding to my 'pictures' till the end of the War, and then when peace comes again I'll be more than delighted to scrub them all off and forget all about it.'

'Have you done anything with that soya flour they're always telling us to use?' I asked.

'Yes, I've tried adding it to ordinary flour, using it to thicken soups and gravy, also in bread and cakes. It has a rather stronger flavour than ordinary flour or cornflour, but I suppose we'll get used to it in time.'

'We are fortunate in having quite a good sized garden, and John is determined to do his little 'dig for victory'. The produce should work another way too in relieving our rather strained finances.'

'That's a very good point', said Mary, 'For none of us these days have much to spare, have we?'

When I returned home, before preparing for the next meal, I did my sums, with the following results:-

ON the 31st July, our very first pay day, John came home clutching the little packet in his hot and sticky hand. A small sum on the face of the envelope gave details of how the final figure was arrived at:-

Wages — £5.7.6 per week		£23.16.0
Plus: Cycle Allowance	10.0	
Boot Allowance	4.0	
Typewriter Allowance	8.0	£ 1. 2.0
		£24.18.0
Less: Pension Fund @ 1/- in the £	1. 2.3	
Widows & Orphans, Insurance etc.	3.0	1. 5.3
The final princely sum		£23.12.9

I worked out a general spending plan for each month, sufficiently elastic to deal with unforseen circumstances. If ever there happened to be a few bob left over, this could be popped into the Bank.

Housekeeping, 4 weeks @ £3 per week	£12. 0.0
Garage, 1 month	10.0
'Phone, 4 weeks rental @ 2/6d. plus calls, say	15.0
Lighting, heating etc.	2. 0.0
Car, running expenses, etc.	7. 0.0
	£22. 5.0

At this rate there would not be much left for clothing and other incidentals, and adjustments would have to be made when neccessary.

Memories of my poor Mother and of the miserable 25/- a week I doled out to her, sometimes grudgingly, from my £5.0.0 salary, still stir my conscience. For this meagre sum she provided me with four good meals a day on seven days a week, a cup of morning call tea, lighting, heating, a well furnished home, laundry, garage, summer sunbathing facilities in her well tended garden, a lounge in which to relax and entertain my friends, and above all, an INDOOR LAV! Yet the only small bonus I ever dreamed of offering her was an occasional visit to our local theatre when I could spare the time. Ah well, maybe some day I'll be able to make up for my youthful thoughtlessness.

In the meantime my practical attention must of necessity be centred around Manorby and all it entailed, including an ever-hungry husband!

My prowess, or otherwise, in the kitchen, left much to be desired, and it seemed I must learn by bitter, sometimes quite dangerous, experience.

I decided one morning to try my hand at an omelette, not from the fresh eggs to which I had been used in days of peace, but from the reconstituted flaky mass we were able periodically to purchase from the grocer.

In the absence of a frying pan or similar shallow receptacle, I put the eggy mixture into my smallest saucepan over a moderate gas flame on the cooker. I left it to cook while I set the table. A rather bright orange flickering shadow, which I took to be the rising sun's reflection, appeared on the kitchen wall. It suddenly grew more and more vivid. I turned round, and to my horror flames were licking from the knife I had inadvertently left in the pan, for the highly flammable knife handle had ignited and in semi-liquid form had overspilled on to the cooker. With great presence of mind I thought, I grabbed the pan and flung the whole lot on to the lawn.

I cleaned up the mess, and settled for toast, marg. and marmalade!

Always ready and willing to try some new recipe, especially if it helped to conserve one or more of the rationed or scarce commodities, I decided to make the new wartime sponge, Victoria style.

The recipe issued by the Ministry of Food suggested substituting liquid paraffin for butter, marg. or other fat. I used the old recipe handed down from my grandmother, but using the equivalent of four eggs from the dried variety, and two tablespoonsful of liquid paraffin.

The final result looked quite good, not very different from the peacetime way. I tried it out on Mary, without divulging the secret ingredients.

'What's the verdict?' I asked after her first bite.

'Well, do you want the whole truth, or shall I just lie and say it's just like Mother used to make?'

'The truth always between friends, please, even if it sometimes hurts a bit.'

'I guess you've been experimenting, and the result is not too bad, but there does seem to be a touch of the oil-can in it,' said Mary, laughing.

I confessed.

'Ugh,' Mary grimaced, 'I though liquid paraffin was only prescribed for the acutely constipated!'

My dear Husband took a more liberal view on tasting the new-fangled cake at teatime.

'Did you enjoy the cake, dear?' I asked as he scoffed the last bite.

'Lovely it was,' he said, 'You can make one of these for me any time.'

Needless to say, many more of these ration saving delights graced our table from time to time.

One of my lesser near failures happened when my Father-in-Law came to spend a few days with us. He, a widower, lived with John's sister, who was a first class cook. I began the process of entertaining the gentleman, filled with apprehension as to my culinary prowess and dexterity.

He arrived just before lunch. We sailed through the meat course, and compliments were rained down on my head. The pudding, however, reduced my spirits to zero.

I gave him a large dollop of what I thought was a deliciously light steamed pudding. It had plopped out of the basin with no trouble at all.

I looked towards him. He appeared to be struggling with his dentures.

'Are you all right?' I asked, tentatively.

'Yes, I'm O.K. Win,' he said with a wry smile. 'I wasn't going to mention it, but since you've asked, I will. My dear, if ever you have a grudge against anyone coming to dine, give them a good helping of fig pudding. It's like trying to chew boulders.'

I suggested biscuits and cheese as a 'peace offering', but he declined. I made a mental note never to offer any dentured friends 'pip' food. As the possessor of my own teeth, it had never occurred to me that even one stray seed can inflict torture when it gets between gum and denture.

One scarcity, unrationed, of which we were becoming increasingly aware, was fish. Cod, salmon, herrings, bloaters, kippers and other types which we had taken for granted in peacetime had almost disappeared from the fishmongers' slabs. In their place we could not fail to notice many new types of small, or larger, piscatorial 'delights', netted from the seas around our shores.

I enquired of our local Fishmonger why so many of his fish were head-less.

'Well you see, dearie' he replied, 'some of them have rather gruesome, catlike, faces, which might put you housewives off, so we behead them and then you still think you're getting the good old fashioned cod and suchlike'.

'What a crafty carry on,' I remarked. 'But I'll try a fillet of that pinky looking stuff over there,' as I pointed towards the back of the slab.

'I'd better tell you what it is,' he offered, 'Just in case you decide against. It's whalemeat, but you can cook it just like any other fish.'

I pictured some poor old whale being spiked, or whatever they do to capture it, and felt sorry it had to happen. But hunger has to take precedence over its tragic end. I took home my latest capture, and John and I enjoyed the end result, and many more similar delicacies later.

I would not like you to think I was the only half of our married partnership to 'get down to it!' John, too, was already doing his share, but most of his leisure activity was confined to our rather long, narrow garden and its possibilities.

'You DIG FOR VICTORY' I advised him, 'and I'll obey the Ministry of

Food's instructions to do my best in the kitchen.'

The garden when we arrived at Manorby, had been sadly neglected, and in July, when we took up residence, it was far too late for summer cultivation. All kinds of weeds - nettles, docks, bindweed, horseradish even - had flourished, unimpeded, often waist high, until John got busy with spade and fork. Before long the whole area was cleared, and a small square prepared for a lawn. The remainder would be devoted to the production of vegetables when sowing and planting time came round towards Autumn and in the following year.

Now John was no stranger to the agricultural scene. In fact, as a young lad in his home village, with a strict gardening enthusiast of a Father, he had been brought up to practical gardening. When quite a small boy, his Dad had a pet rule:- GARDEN FIRST, PLAY LATER MY BOY. As a budding young sportsman, little Johnnie often resented his Pa's insistence, especially when he could hear the cricket, or football, being tossed around the field adjoining the family garden. Yet, he is the first to admit that his early training there was to prove invaluable as the war and all its scarcities continued.

While John was busy outside, I was quite content to do my indoor chores, though occasionally, on grabbing duster and mop to collect the previous day's deposit on furniture, ledges and stairs, and it seemed everywhere else, near panic would assail me. One particular day remains in my memory more forcibly than the rest. I was feeling rather tired and slightly fed-up for no apparent special reason.

'Good Heavens,' I reflected, 'I'll have to be doing this every day to eternity, cooking, washing-up, laundering, bed-making and.... and.... There's no end to it.'

The unwelcome words of Mr. HCO's forecast of doom came to mind, and refused to be dispelled. Perhaps he knew me better than I knew myself when he said:-

'You're not cut out for skivvying and domestic drudgery, you'll never get used to two-up-two-down-lav-in-the-backyard living. Before you know where you are, you'll have six snotty nosed little kids milling round you, driving you mad. Don't say I haven't warned you. You'll be trapped in the bread-and-dripping syndrome with never a cat in Hell's chance of escape. In six months you'll be back here on your knees begging to return to the job you do best.'

'Oh dear me,' I thought, for I was really temporarily feeling quite miserable. 'Well, at least he was wrong in one respect — we are three-up-three-down, even though the Lav. prediction did happen to be correct.'

'Perhaps some day we'll get the chance of a move — and an indoor you-know-what,' a thought which gave my spirits the up-turn they sadly needed.

I switched on the wireless, hoping its music would enliven my downcast thoughts. It invariably did, and this was no exception. The orchestra was playing what had become our own theme tune — Dvorak's Humoresque. Memories flooded back of my first evening out with the new found Copper pal. After all, trying to keep our two selves well fed and happy must be our game of life, our destiny, to be played not with backward glances, but with hope for our future.

A challenge such as this must be well worth while.

CHAPTER 3

Bombs in Paradise — and Elsewhere

The Air Raid Precautions Report Centre was situated in the Manor House, almost opposite Manorby. It seemed natural, that living so close and married to a Police Sergeant, I should be invited to join the team of Clerks who had volunteered to assist in taking down telephone messages and making themselves generally useful.

It was the Controller who called one day shortly after Mary had invited me to share her shelter.

'We wondered if you could possibly spare the time to join us for duty occasionally?' he asked so hesitantly that I felt almost certain he expected me to turn down the offer.

'Yes, of course I'd like to come along, especially as John, my Husband, has to turn out for duty on every alert, and I'm left alone. As a matter of fact, I've just been asked to share a shelter down the road, but to do something really useful I feel is a duty no-one in my position should ignore.'

'How about coming across now, and I'll introduce you to those on duty,' he suggested.

'Yes, I'm quite free until teatime,' and off we went.

On arrival I was shown round the Office, and met about seven men and women, most of whom were manning a telephone.

My hours of duty were arranged, with the added proviso that I was at liberty to join the staff at any time during an air raid alert.

I had already done several tours of afternoon duty, when one evening, following MM's clarion call, I was sitting at my desk, chatting to one of my colleagues, when my 'phone rang.

On picking up the receiver, the voice at the other end of the line shouted so loudly and excitedly I could scarcly hear what he was trying to tell me.

My ear drums fairly rattled as he yelled:-

'There's been a stick of incendiary bombs dropped in Paradise.'

'Paradise?' I queried.

'Yes, PARADISE, P for Peter, A for apple, etc.'

'Where on earth's Paradise,' I asked him.

'It's not up in Heaven,' he bawled, 'It's back of No Man's Lane, between the Rectory and Barbadoes.'

'Barbadoes?' I enquired, 'That's in the West Indies.'

'I don't want a bloody geography lesson, thank you,' he retorted. 'Time's precious, and you're being bloody awkward.'

I paused as I nudged the elbow of the clerk sitting next to me.

'Anything wrong?' she asked.

'Well, there's some old boy on my 'phone who's talking about bombs in Paradise near Barbadoes. I think he must be a bit tiddley, or he's having me on.'

She moved over to my instrument, saying as she did so:-

'There are such places, I'll explain later.'

She took down the message from an irate Warden, explaining as she did so that I was new to the district and lacked local knowledge.

I passed the information to the right department, who dealt expeditiously with the fires which had begun to take hold of parts of the local countryside.

During a slight lull in aerial and telephone activity which followed, she explained that Paradise was the name of a certain field some three miles from our town, and Barbadoes was a very tiny hamlet nearby. Apparently BARBADOES, (note the extra letter E) was christened by two brothers who, having made their fortune in the West Indies, returned to their native heath, and celebrated their success by building a row of cottages, naming the small colony Barbadoes. History had not recorded, however, the reason the extra letter E had slipped on to the sculpted nameplate attached to the brickwork above the central cottage.

Our town, being largely of an industrial nature, always seemed to us to be a potential target for enemy aircraft. I did not expect anything drastic to happen, however, one peaceful Sunday afternoon.

I was sitting scarcely thigh-deep in my regulation five inches of lovely caressing hot water bath, singing 'There'll Always be an England' my favourite Pop song of the day, thoroughly wallowing in my once-weekly soap and soak, when suddenly I heard the most earth shattering and uncomfortably close thud-thud-thud.

I sat tight for a second or two, my ears cocked in case I might detect the sound of approaching enemy aircraft. Yes, quite distinctly came the dread droning, the unmistakable sound of Jerry's do-badders.

'Strange,' I thought, 'I didn't hear MM, but decided my noisy bath taps must have drowned even her moans.'

It suddenly occurred to me that the target might have been our local Ironworks at the bottom of the town. Still half wet after a quick towel down, I dressed at top speed, went downstairs and awaited further noise.

John arrived late for tea, which was not unusual these days.

'What were all those heavy thuds I heard this afternoon?' I asked.

'I only heard one, the others must have been your imagination.'

Not wishing to argue and my curiosity making me impatient, I asked him, 'What was that one then?'

'A bomb fell into one side of the Canal, causing quite a crater but no damage otherwise.'

'Thank goodness' was my relieved reply, although still confident that there were three bumps.

I was not surprised, therefore, when John announced after his next duty was over that three bombs had dropped close to the main road, one of which had demolished the end of a semi-detached house. By a miracle nobody was there, but one of the beds was suspended dangerously over the space where a wall had collapsed.

Compared with so many big and smaller towns in this Country, we were quite fortunate in experiencing only sporadic aerial visits from the enemy.

Several weeks after this incident, John received a 'phone message at home stating that something had fallen from the skies and penetrated the roof of a house, whose occupants were also out at the time.

At once he donned jacket, tin hat, gas mask and all the other accoutrements necessary for duty, and sped away on his two wheeled steed to investigate. Many hours later he returned home, looking rather drained.

'Whatever has kept you all this time?' I asked, worried in case he had been involved in a serious situation.

'Phew! I've had a literally hair-raising experience.'

'Was it a bomb?'

'It was too — a whopper. We thought at first it must have been a large piece of shrapnel that had fallen through the roof. When we entered the living room we were left in no doubt at all. Do you know that missile had passed right through the centre of the dining table, leaving on its downward flight a large bomb-girth sized, neatly cut hole, some sixteen inches in diameter, with a matching hole in the earth beneath. The cavity I should say was between twelve and fifteen feet deep. And after all that it had failed to explode.'

'What happened then?'

'We contacted the Bomb Disposal Squad, who arrived within a few minutes of receiving our alert. They inspected the scene, expressing surprise that the weapon had made such a clean departure southwards finishing up slightly horizontally as it came to the end of its journey.'

'Oh dear, if I'd known you were so close to it, I'd have had a fit.'

'Don't ever worry yourself. We always take every precaution, and if any of us happen to meet our Waterloo, then in wartime we all have to make the best of it — at least those who are left behind.'

'How did the BDS men deal with it then?'

'They dug a big hole, much wider than the bomb itself, then began the risky job of de-fusing it. They began very gingerly but in dead earnest. We were all deathly silent. You could have heard the proverbial pin drop. Suddenly there was a high pitched 'ping'. All but the unfortunate men down the hole took steps backward, hoping the bomb had not decided after all to blow us to eternity.'

'The suspense must have been horrific.'

The BDS men stopped stock still for a brief moment, then called to us at the top:-

'Don't worry, chaps, it was only a little stone that had slipped from the pile of earth above.'

'What a relief it must have been,' said I.

'Relief, my word. Anyway, the operation continued without further excitement, and at last with baited breath, and I suspect a prayer from the believers among us, a voice from the depths announced:- 'O.K. fellahs, we've defused the bloody thing.'

The offending instrument of potential destruction was then raised to the surface and removed for examination.

CHAPTER 4

Bobbies, Boozers and Bad Lads

As an ambitious young Police Constable John had decided that if ever he reached the rank of Sergeant, or even higher up the scale of promotion, he would concentrate on giving all the help and advice he could to any shy, inexperienced officer with whom he worked. This decision stemmed largely from the fact that in the early days of his service, and sometimes later, he had really suffered through the impatience, sarcasm and bullying dished out to him by some, certainly not all, senior officers who often expected old heads on young shoulders, with apparently no notion that a little help here and a little encouragement there goes such a long way towards instilling confidence and competence, knowledge and resourcefulness in their juniors.

John's practical application of this maxim was brought home to me when he told me of a group of newly engaged Constables who had just arrived in the town. They came from the Highlands of Scotland, some had never even seen, or travelled on, a train before making the journey southwards, and all were apprehensive and sometimes homesick. Following several weeks' instruction in the County Police School, it was not surprising that some of them at least were quite overwhelmed at the prospect of having to deal with any one of the thousands of accidents, crimes and other happenings that came their way, and look efficient to the public.

'Seems pretty cruel to me, leaving them to their own devices too soon after such a short period of training,' I said, my sympathies as always with the underdog.

'Not quite as bad as it may sound. For the first few days a new man is on duty he is accompanied by a more experienced officer, then they are on their own, commonsense their best ally.'

'I'd be tempted to turn a blind eye to something I felt I couldn't tackle, perhaps dash round the corner and pretend I hadn't seen it.'

'My word, you'd be in dire trouble if you did.'

This particular batch of young greenhorns settled down quite quickly. Their integration problem was soon considerably relieved as they became acquainted with the very attractive young ladies living in or near the town. The smart uniform worked like a magnet, coupled with the fascinating lilt of the Scottish accent.

On arriving home for lunch one day, John said laughingly:- 'Had a bit of fun, or perhaps I should say trouble, with one of the young Scots this morning.'

'Oh dear, nothing serious, I hope.'

'Not for me, but for young Mac it was pretty terrifying. You see, Court day sometimes makes an experienced Officer a little nervous when entering the witness box. It was a new ordeal for this young man who was so awe inspired and tongue-tied, unable to find any words to express himself, that he persisted in kicking the woodwork in front of him, in the misguided hope perhaps that this kind of carry on would somehow force the words to come, and Heaven knows, he'd practised them again and again with me before he entered the Courtroom.'

'Keep your feet still,' commanded the austere looking Magistrate, 'we don't want percussion added to the proceedings.'

'There was relief all round as poor Mac recovered his composure and with a couple of promptings, sotto voce he managed to spit out his evidence.'

'Thank goodness,' I thought, asking:-

'Any more excitement this happy morn?'

'Only one slight hitch when another Constable of the same group, having learned to recite his evidence parrot fashion, forgot his 'lines' in the middle, coming to a full stop, to the obvious irritation of the Beak. However, he managed to struggle through it in the end.'

The Court House, incidentally, was no purpose built edifice, but simply one of the upstairs rooms in the Town Hall, situated almost opposite the Police Station and facing the Market Place. When not occupied by Legal Eagles and Sinners, the same room doubled up as a Dance Hall, Conference Room or a multitude of other uses. The rest of the building comprised Council Offices, the Mayor's Parlour, several Loo's, M. & F.

The list of Magistrates included representatives from a fair cross section of the local trades and professions, all of whom took their turn in dealing with local wrong-doers.

Our Town, typical of most of similar size and population, was policed by the Superintendent and around thirty-six male personnel of the regular Force, and some ten War Reserve Constables who, in peacetime followed other occupations. Two lady clerks completed the staff. There was also a Special Inspector, a Sergeant and about twenty Special Constables, who did a wonderful job in many ways, often relieving the pressures of the regular Officers on traffic control, visits to Air Raid Warden's Posts, conducting school children across busy roads, and generally supplementing and alleviating their work.

Towards efficient policing of the town, it was divided into a series of beats, along which were specific places known as 'Points.' If ever a Constable was found to have missed a Point, unless he had good reason to do so, he was reported to HQ, and duly reprimanded.

My life was destined to be spent at a distance of about three-quarters of a mile from the Police Station, and thus did not give me any opportunity of seeing at first hand the goings and comings, the triumphs and tribulations, crime and criminals. My information came directly from John, or from one or other of his colleagues who were not slow to realise that a cup of tea at Mrs. B's was always acceptable to a plodding Copper.

John's tours of duty provided him with a multitude of tasks, some quite exciting, others of a routine, less spectacular, nature. But all gave us plenty of talking points when he returned home.

One of his duties was to visit the numerous Air Raid Wardens' Posts dotted around and in the town. These were often situated in factories and warehouses.

Some were made reasonably warm and comfortable, others were just the opposite.

Personnel consisted of a wide variety of people, many drawn from their own area, some over the age for National Service. There was one particularly outstanding member of a certain Post not far from the town centre, who recorded the Warden's duties, with tongue in cheek, as follows:-

'There's a mystic set of creatures who are joined to A.R.P.
Called 'Wardens' by the hoi-polloi and by the powers that be,
But when the sentry's planted and there's no-one on the ground,
And heads are drawn together, and the bottle's going round,
When the gas is burning dimly, then contention sharpened wits
Admit that they are merely just a set of bloody twits.

For if there's aught wants doing that requires but little brains,
Such as filling flipping sandbags, or censusing the cats,
Or popping round with ear-plugs, or emptying the drains,
Or changing 'smalls' for 'mediums', or diapers on brats,
The Council calls the Wardens, whose solemn conclave sits
And approves of the instructions, since they know they're nought but twits.

And when the trouble's over, and bouquets are handed round,
And someone gets the OBE with all expenses found,
And this one gets the DSO, and that one gets a Cross,
And another gets a knighthood, making profit out of loss,
Our friend will get an armband and lots of little bits
Such as whistle and report pad - the very thing for — TWITS!

Another of John's duties was to pay regular visits to the local Public Houses, and one afternoon during a walk up the main shopping street, I could not help noticing that our town was well blessed, or sometimes perhaps cursed, with them.

When John came home at teatime, I remarked:- 'Do you know, I counted eight Pubs in Main Street during my shopping safari today.'

'That's just about a quarter of the whole number scattered around the town,' he replied. 'There are in fact forty-eight of them, no less, and that's not counting quite a number of off-licensed shops.

'What's the population then?'

'Around 35,000 at the last count, I believe.'

'That gives one pub for every 730 folk' said I, doing a rapid mental calculation — not my forte as a rule!

Not to be outdone, or out-mathematised, John added:- 'And if you take the total acreage of about 3,000, that allows for one pub every 64 acres or thereabouts.'

'I wonder how many Churches we have?'

'About fifteen, I would say. To save racking your brains, that means one church to every three pubs and two thousand three hundred people.'

'Splendid. Go to the top of the Class!'

'I guess the church congregations increase as the war news worsens.' I remarked.

'They always do, but the Pubs still have the greater clientele. Their Prayer Books have handles, you know.'

'Ha-ha! Somehow I don't think you're the first one to voice it.'

'When I first came here I was quite surprised at the names of some of our 'Locals'. Local Landowner, the Duke of Rutland is perpetuated in the Rutland Hotel and the Rutland Cottage Inn. The Mundy Arms recalls the Mundy family, benefactors in many ways to the Miners whose Pits they owned. The Colliers themselves are not forgotten in The Miners Arms, and the Jolly Colliers.'

A slight pause followed as John collected his thoughts.

'Tell me more. I'm fascinated.'

Well, there's the Stanton Hotel, used largely by employees of nearby Stanton Ironworks, and they haven't forgotten The Needlemakers, reminiscent of another local industry, hosiery. Farming too is established by The Harrow Inn, The White Cow and the Durham Ox. With two railway stations in the town, one almost expects the Bridge Inn and The Great Northern, both very popular ports of call. Then the aesthetic sense of the townsfolk is not forgotten in The Royal Oak, The Sevenoaks and The Poplar Inns.'

Another pause.

'Any more,?' I asked, wondering why, having worked for ten years at a Brewery, I had not made a study of pub names in my home town and county.

'We're getting near the end, but must not leave out another popular pastime here, The Trumpet Inn, reminds us of the affection of so many musical people in the town. Brass Bands were a great feature in the local Parks. I almost forgot The Hand and Heart, and The Live and Let Live, a reminder of the general honesty and tolerance of all. There's only one more I can think of, and that's The Gallows Inn, almost a guarantee to deter any homicidal inclinations of the population, reminding one and all of the ultimate penalty for the ultimate crime.'

'If you weren't such a good Copper, I think you'd make a first class teacher!'

'One of my regular jobs' continued John, is to inspect all the public houses periodically, to ensure that no-one is caught gaming, playing for money, or holding an illegal betting slip in his hot little hand. Those discovered have to be reported and suffer the consequence of such brash folly.'

'I should have thought there were more serious things for you and your colleagues to deal with these wartime days. These offences do seem rather trivial to me. I really thought your visits of inspection came down to an Officer nipping in through the back door of a pub, swallowing a crafty pint on the Landlord, chatting up the buxom barmaid, signing the record book, and then up and away to the next port of call.'

'You must be joking. The Law must be obeyed. Even if a modest half pint of beer is dispensed after the official closing time, Mine Host is really in trouble.'

The next day, John was on early duty, that is 5 a.m. to 9 a.m. He arrived home at 11.

'Sorry I'm a bit late,' he said apologetically.

'A bit? But carry on. What is it this time?'

'A barrel of beer has been pinched from the yard at the rear of one of the Pubs. They suspect a group of late-ish drinkers who had left a bit on the merry side. I went to see one of them at his home. I knew him slightly and as I thought him the weakest link in the chain, decided to see him first.'

'Any luck?'

'Yes. He began to shake, when I questioned him, at the thought of being in trouble, but his excuses were so contradictory that after only a few questions, he confessed. He gave me a bonus too by giving me the names and addresses of his accomplices.'

'That's good news — another crime solved.'

'Wait a bit, you've not heard the sequel yet. Word had somehow got around to his pals, who quickly buried the cask with contents in some allotment gardens — to be exhumed later and consumed at their leisure, or so they thought, when suspicion had died down. They completely misjudged our tenacity. After strenuously denying all involvement, they admitted the offence which they pleaded was more of a prank than a wish to steal the ale.'

'What happened to the barrel? They ought to give it to the Police as a reward.'

'We wouldn't be allowed to accept it. No, it was replaced into the pub's stock, apparently none the worse for its interment.'

Petrol rationing gave many a policeman and private citizen more than a slight headache.

One day, John accompanied by one of the Constables was 'walking and cycling the beat', keeping their eyes wide open as usual, when they both noticed a well known local car being driven well away from the course for which his petrol ration was allowed.

'We motioned to him to stop,' said John, but he just accelerated, hoping no doubt that his speed would prevent our seeing his dimmed number plate. We jumped on our bikes which we had left leaning up against a wall, and gave chase, knowing that we could not possibly catch him up. Being fairly certain we knew the culprit, we approached his home as silently as pussycats, in carpet slippers.'

'Good for you. What then?'

'No good Copper goes direct to the house of a suspect. Instead we very stealthily entered his garage which, fortunately for us, was unlocked. There was a lovely warm smell. We felt the car's bonnet. It warmed our chilly hands. We then knocked at the house door. After several minutes it was opened. There stood our suspect, rubbing his eyes, yawning widely, dressed in pyjamas. 'What the Hell's the matter?' he asked us, stifling yet another yawn. 'I was fast asleep. Fancy knocking me up at this time. It's gone eleven.'

John continued:- 'We have reason to believe you have only just returned home in your car, having travelled along an area other than your permitted one.'

'But I haven't been out in the car all week,' he persisted.

'Then who has?' asked John. 'Would it surprise you if I told you the car engine is still warm?'

After further weak excuses, and on hearing that he had been recognised off course, he finally admitted his misdemeanour. He said he had obliged a sick friend by taking him home.'

'Will he be prosecuted,' I asked.

'Yes, he will, and probably fined quite heavily.'

'That's that then,' I said. 'Another heinous crime solved.'

'You'll laugh when I tell you the sequel,' added John, the following day.

'That same man was outside his house this afternoon when a Constable and I walked past. Go and ask him if he'll buy a ticket for the Police Ball next week,' I told him, as I walked away.

After several minutes the Constable caught up with me.

'Any luck?' I asked.

'Yes, he bought two, after he'd asked me 'Did HE send you?' And when I said yes, he said with feeling 'It's like his bloody cheek!''

John explained to me something of Police powers in time of war as regards potential law breakers.

'We are allowed to immobilise any car or other vehicle suspected of being off course, illegally parked, or otherwise disobeying the law. Sometimes we remove the rotor arm, let down the tyres, or use some other effective means, like a swift wee-wee into the petrol tank.'

'I sometimes think you're a lot of spoil sports.'

'Any other special wartime hazards?' I asked.

'Oh yes, lots. If we look like having a thin day at Court, we have only to keep our eyes skinned for black-out offences. Nothing like the odd few cases to make people more careful about showing even the slightest chink of light, and it all helps to keep our crimes solved figures on the up and up.'

'Anything in this line lately?' I asked.

'Yes. Only the other evening when walking down Main Street the whole road was lit by a brilliant blaze of light coming from one of the large shops. I dashed across the road and plunged my tough toecapped, legging-topped boot right through one of the glass panels of a door. I found the main electric light switch, and out went the beacon.'

'Are you allowed to enter a shop without a member of the staff present?' I enquired, thinking of possible temptation to nick something.

'Certainly we are in an emergency such as that. You don't stand on ceremony when a Jerry 'plane might spot it. The Manager was contacted while I waited just outside the shop in case anyone passing might have had wicked plans.'

He told me of another incident which proved to be somewhat embarrassing both to the miscreants and to John himself.

'I was walking along one of the side streets,' he said, 'When I spied a narrow shaft of light coming through the darkness across the pavement, from a small house, one of the prevalent off-the-sidewalk-into-the-parlour types. The light was coming through a niche in the front door which was illfitting through warping of the wood. I tried the door handle, and to my surprise it was unlocked. I called out 'Is anyone there?' as I stepped inside. Imagine my surprise when I saw a vision in pretty pink nightie lying in bed with her spouse — at least I hope it was. Obviously she didn't have a headache!'

'Naughty, naughty! I can guess what they were up to.'

'Well, when we had all recovered slightly from our confusion, I explained as quickly as I could about the light.'

'You won't summons us, will you, we're very sorry,' said the male of the union.

'I ought to report you really, but I'm no spoil sport,' I said, to their obvious relief. If you'll promise me to get that door fixed, or at least blacked out, I'll let you off with this verbal caution. But don't go and tell all your friends, or they'll think they can get away with it too, and I can't guarantee it!'

Crime generally in our town and its environs was considered to be no worse than in most other similar communities. Juvenile delinquents, perhaps the most disturbing of all, were alas on the increase, as the busy Thursday afternoon Courts devoted to them so often revealed. For these judicial appearances, all Police Officers wore civilian clothes, the idea behind this being to put the young culprits at their ease! I could never quite see the reasoning behind this rule, particularly as, when the youngsters get as far as the Court, most of them couldn't care less whether the Officers wore uniform or their long Johns!

However, it was not up to me to criticise the set up. My interest, as always, was in hearing the latest news from the Courts, whether Juvenile or Adult. In fact I was rapidly developing a nose for news.

John arrived late for lunch one day, ate his meal with one eye on the clock, changed into his lounge suit, gave me a quick peck on the cheek, saying:-

'Juvenile Court this afternoon. Musn't keep the little darlings waiting,' and off he sped on his bike.

He returned some five hours later, looking tired and rather frustrated.

'These Magistrates give me the willies,' he said as he sat down in the kitchen. 'You'd think, wouldn't you, they'd see their function as that of trying the youngster-wrong-doer. Not a bit of it. Most of them seem interested in deeply interrogating the Police Officer while the guilty one stands grinning during the procedure. You would not believe what some of these youngsters get away with. More often than not, the Magistrate, with a benign smile on his face looks the youngster in the eye, saying something like 'Now you won't do it again, will you Sonny, or I shall have to get really cross with you,' or, 'Now this time I'm going to forgive you, so try and do useful things instead of getting into trouble,' etc. etc.'

To a Policeman, after all the trouble he has taken to discover a culprit, it's more than disheartening to see some of these young thugs and thieves leaving the Courtroom feeling proud of their achievement, when they should at least *look* penitent.'

'But they don't all get away with it, do they? How about those who are despatched to Remand Homes and similar places?' I asked.

'No, but too many of them do, in my opinion. There was one lad today who received 'the treatment'. Aged fifteen years, scruffy in appearance, obviously arrogant, aggressive and completely unashamed, he appeared on a number of charges for theft, truancy and other anti-social misdemeanours.'

'We can't do a thing with him,' moaned his Dad.

'Nothing', enchoed his Mum.

'We've given him everything we could,' added Dad.

'Everything', repeated his harassed Mum.

The magistrate, wrapped in thought for a few moments, thinking no doubt that the lad's doting parents had denied him the very thing he needed most — DISCIPLINE —, broke his silence with:

'You'll go to a Remand Home for six months. During that time I want you to promise me you will obey all the rules, learn whatever you can while you have the opportunity, making yourself useful in every way. I do not wish to see you before me ever again. Your future is in your own hands. By the end of your period of living away from your own home, you should have learned of all the advantages of living honestly among all our other law abiding citizens. Now go away, and use this six months — YOU'LL NEVER GET A BETTER CHANCE.'

'His Mother screamed, Dad did his ineffective best to console her, as the lad was led away to begin his remedial treatment,' added John.

'That should cool his criminal ardour,' I suggested.

'If anything will. He's such a tough young nut.'

I could not help remarking to John one day after he had attended a busy session in Court:

'I shall never understand why so many people prefer to take to crime, when to me it seems so much easier to lead a normal life. I can't think of anything worse than being hunted by the Police.'

'That doesn't bother them, particularly the hardened criminal. In fact, they regard dodging the Law and its Officers as the most exciting part of the exercise. Who knows, perhaps when the War is over, some Scientist will come up with something which has the power to convert a criminal mind into a normal one. On second thoughts, if ever they do, think of all the Coppers who'll be made redundant!'

CHAPTER 5

Pregnant Pause — and a Honeymoon for Three

'I think I'm pregnant, don't faint, 'I announced as we sat down to breakfast one morning in early December, just four and a half months after we were wed.

'Phew, you've made me go all hot. How do you know?'

'Well, I'm not certain yet, but I've looked it up in the Medical Book, and I seem to have most of the signs and symptoms, plus a few it doesn't mention.'

'You'd better get busy and see the Doctor, in case you need some special sort of treatment,' suggested an anxious John.

'All in good time, but my Mum never had any pills or potions over her eight, so I don't anticipate any trouble, not yet anyway.'

We had discussed the question of having children, taking into account the fact that John at forty-two and I at thirty-three might conceivably have passed the age of tolerance, energy even, so essential in the upbringing of a youngster. Nevertheless, in spite of our ages and the doubtful pleasure and pain of bringing a new little soul into such a troubled world, we had decided to leave it all to Mother Nature.

For several days I had been feeling rather below par, particularly during the mornings when, even my usually welcome husband-borne early morn cup of tea seemed repulsive, and the very thought of cooking breakfast even produced a strange kind of nausea, quite foreign to my normal healthy appetite.

I visited the Doctor, who told me that although it was rather early to diagnose definite pregnancy, he would confirm it or otherwise if I would visit him again about a month hence, say shortly after Christmas.

In the meantime, he suggested a morning potion of glucose powder and water, which sometimes worked, but more often did not.

Preparations for Christmas did succeed in taking my mind off my condition and hope that I was pregnant, for at this stage I began to look forward to a happy event.

I began with the cake and puddings made loosely from my Grandmother's recipes adapted to wartime shortages. Dried prunes, of which I had managed to get a whole pound, with some sultanas I had saved up, constituted the fruit content, grated raw carrot and potato helped add to the bulk, and some black treacle from 'under the Grocer's counter', together with a little of our precious sugar ration and flour made a mixture not too dissimilar to the original confection. All three puddings were boiled in the gas copper, this being the only receptacle big enough to accommodate them simultaneously. The fact that the kitchen walls were running with fatty steam during the process did not worry me too much, as John came to the rescue with soap and water.

One of the local farmers promised us a chicken for Christmas dinner, and John assured me he knew a good place to nick some berried holly for decoration.

'What if the farmer cops you taking his holly?' I asked, anxious to keep within the law.

'He'll never miss it, but it's woe betide anyone else caught helping himself.'

'I knew Coppers didn't always practise what they preach,' was my slight reprimand.

'If it makes you happy, I'll ASK him for some.'

'You know best.'

Christmas Day arrived, John having forewarned me that he would have to spend some of the day on duty, but the Superintendent had promised all the lads they could spend dinnertime at home.

We sat down to our 'sumptuous' spread. John carved the bird, and suddenly my tummy revolted. I could not face it, not even a tiny morsel of its tender breast. I dissolved into tears as John made short work of his well loaded plates.

'Never mind,' he said consolingly, 'Tell you what. Why not keep your dinner till teatime, when perhaps you'll feel better.'

I did as he suggested, and at 5.30 p.m. I yaffled the lot!

Our first Christmas, in spite of my lunchtime lapse, passed very happily. Our neighbours were out for the day, so John and I had a little concert to my rather second rate piano accompaniment, the programme including the recently popular 'White Christmas', several Carols, and John's favourite songs, 'The Windmill', 'Come to the Fair,' 'A Bachelor Gay,' (not any more, he wasn't!) and 'The Floral Dance.'

Fortunately for us all, Hitler and his satellites left us in peace for the whole Christmas period. W.S. Gilbert's song, 'A Policeman's Lot is Not a Happy One,' certainly did not apply to JCB at this stage in our partnership.

I made a further visit to the Doctor towards mid-January 1941, and my suspicions were confirmed. He gave me the usual advice about not over-eating, yet taking plenty of exercise and rest.

I walked home, my feet hardly touching the ground. John was at home.

'It's true, it's true,' I exclaimed excitedly.

'Aren't we lucky,' he said, as thrilled as I was.

During my pregnant pause, life for me passed peacefully, with not too many urgent dashes over the way to the A.R.P. Centre, other than my normal duty times there. Housework, shopping and cooking took up a good deal of my time, and I was never bored.

Most days were crowned with the prospect of a good story on John's return from duty, as he updated me with details of current events, some quite trivial, others more exciting.

I was grateful for this rapport for, as the wife of a serving Officer of the Law I was not allowed to take on a job of work outside the home. We were living very much in the era of 'A wife's place is in the home, performing the full-time career of caring for husband and family,' and I was never allowed to forget it!

Shortage of cash was in some way compensated for by the fact that we were not alone in this. With careful spending we managed to keep solvent — just.

During most afternoons I turned my attention to sewing and knitting. On the former I was never at all keen, having in my more opulent single days gladly joined the 'throw away not worth mending' brigade. Now it was different, and I even began to enjoy needlework.

In the past my sisters and I had often laughed at Mother as she sat for hours, apparently enjoying herself, darning, mending, her own and our brothers' socks, vests and other wearing apparel. She would say simply:-

'Yes, my girls, you'll laugh on the other side of your faces one day. Just you wait till you're wed!'

Sure enough that time had now arrived — with a vengeance.

Was it I who was about to transform a wide roll of unbleached calico, purchased for threepence a yard, into a pair of off-white sheets? (The market stallholder had assured me it would go white after several boilings).

Was it really I who was about to turn several of the older sheets from John's former home, sides to middle, as Mother had so often done? Was it really I who produced dishcloths, floorcloths and dusters from odds and ends now too precious to discard?

It was. Sometimes I would pause in amazement at my own versatility. Was this queen of invention, adaptation and improvisation really me?

In peacetime the contents of my clothes line today would have raised many an eyebrow, but now we all had similar picturesque clothing pegged thereon. Mine had blue shirts with floral tails, white shirts with pink tails, fancy pants, male and female, with gaily coloured gussets, all blowing in the washday breeze. We were all in the same poverty club, but it was shortage of coupons and money which caused this scenic change.

One of my masterpieces was a skirt made from an old pair of John's worsted trousers. It was surprising how an empty unbleached cotton 1-cwt. sugar bag, handed to me on the quiet by Grocer Fred, was changed after being flattened out, washed, and embellished with rows of different coloured bias bindings, into a tablecloth. Further gifts of this nature became tea towels, curtains, hankies even.

Knitting wool, very scarce and coupon-bound, gave another excuse for improvision. As a keen knitter, I set to work unravelling several jumpers and cardigans I had made, whose elbows and other parts were worn. The crinkly produce was then skeined, washed and rewound into balls. A rather laborious procedure, but the re-knitted garments made the exercise well worth while.

Why the odd shirt tails, you may ask. As so often happens, the collars wear and become threadbare while the rest of the garment is good. It was not too difficult to unpick the original collars, using the old one as a pattern, lop off the shirt tail, cut out a newish one, machine it together and attach it to the neck, then rummage in the bit bag for something to substitute for the tail.

And all the time my pregnant pause was going from strength to strength, or perhaps it could be more correctly described as going from skinny to rotund!

The troublesome morning sickness had disappeared long before Easter and, apart from several rather unusual 'cravings', all went well. I developed a strong yearning for a kipper, and as these had almost disappeared from the fish shops, I had to make do with any other kind of fish. The trouble was I fancied them RAW. Another of my strange desires was COAL. I would pick a nice bright cobble and gnaw away. Perhaps the most unusual of my fancies was Sloan's Liniment. This lotion was a favourite cold cure used by my Mother on any member of the family who suffered from sneezes and wheezes. Peppery, vinegary, breathtaking, extremely painful if dropped by accident on certain vulnerable parts of the body, it was recommended for external use only. My passion began with gentle sniffs at the bottle, followed by a few drops on my tongue, and several sips. It burned my throat, burned the route to my stomach, rather like an extra helping of strong curry, but still I craved for more. That is until one day I confided my trouble in Mary:-

'I wish I could kick the habit', I told her.

'You'd better do just that. What about little Fred? It might harm him, don't you think?' she advised.

(John and I had sometimes referred to our unborn infant as Fred, although boy or girl we knew would be equally welcome to make our duet into a trio).

Commonsense prevailed. I poured the rest of the contents of that bottle away, and with it all craving for anything disappeared quite miraculously.

By the end of May I was not alone in working towards fruition. John had already been working hard in the garden. All this slogging we hoped would also bear fruit — and veg. — before long.

In the past I had often done a little moan about his daytime police duties, with split shifts, that is, spreading the eight hours over twelve. In other words, when he went on at 5 a.m. off at 9 a.m., on again at 1 p.m. and off at 5 p.m. for two weeks, then he would change for a further two weeks to on at 9 a.m. off at 1 p.m., on again at 5 p.m. and off at 9 p.m. Mealtimes had to be adjusted accordingly.

His night duty for the fifth and sixth weeks was worked eight hours at one go, from 9 p.m. to 5 a.m.

All duty times were, of course, subject to anything unexpected that might crop up to detain him — and this was quite often.

However, this Spring was no time for grumbling on my part, for his off duty periods proved invaluable to the garden. Having cleaned the weed ridden ground last Autumn, he enjoyed the task ahead.

When the weather was warm I sat in the garden, partly to keep John company, but always my busy fingers were making something old into new.

I was lucky one day to hear that our local needlework shop had a supply of 2-ply white wool, admirably suited to baby wear. I dashed up to purchase some, and was given a whole pound at a price of 6d. (2p.) an ounce.

A shawl for the babe was my priority, and in just over three weeks my knitting needles completed not only a large shawl, but also a smaller head wrap, and three matinee coats.

My sewing machine, given to me by the family on my twenty-first birthday, was proving a boon. When it was not running hot on the make-do-and-mend exercise, it was ploughed into service making baby things. I managed to get most of the material for six baby nighties, and terry towelling sufficient for three dozen nappies at threepence a yard.

May came and went, and June brought a still bigger and better (I hope) Winifred. My weight, in spite of reasonable care over diet, just romped up, my 'umble umbelicus, formerly a shell-like beauty, had completely flattened out, and my waistline was impossible to define. Three stone up and two months to go. Oh Lord, what a weight to carry around!

I visited the local Maternity Home, Parkhyrst (not to be confused with Parkhurst, the Penitentiary of similar name). The building, a large detached house, was well appointed for its purpose of bringing into the world the next generation.

My bed was booked for an elastic date around the 17th August. Until then I was told to make a monthly visit to ensure that all was well with US.

By the end of the eighth month, so colossal were my vital statistics that it was only with the utmost difficulty I could bend forwards, or even sideways. I developed a complaint which John and I dubbed 'dropsomania'. That is, things just slipped out of my hands usually floorwards. He would come home to find the ground littered with knives, forks, dusters, soap and other things on which I had lost my grip.

A visit to my Doctor in early August assured me all was well so far. After palpating my 'interesting' part, my huge domelike tum, he said:-

'I think he'll be a chip off the old block — I can feel his Copper's feet.'

Right or wrong will be proved.

August 15th found me brimful of energy. I cleaned out several cupboards, rearranged several pieces of light furniture, dusted the books and bookcase, and felt on top of the world.

Came early morning on the 16th, and several slight twinges towards the rear of the 'dome' seemed unusual, but perhaps it was an attack of wind. I rose as usual, did my chores including the preparation and cooking of lunch. John returned to the Office, having been alerted by me as to the possibility of making a quick dash to Parkhyrst.

Teatime came and went, but by then things were really hotting up, and so was I. By eight o'clock I was duly installed in the Home, John having transported me. I must admit I felt more inwardly calm than his outward countenance showed.

In spite of this, however, when faced with something of a crisis, I inevitably have an attack of migraine. This was no exception. However, five hours later my tiny pink squealing little girl was born.

I slept the sleep of the 'hereafter', and awoke feeling wonderfully fit, to find two more new Mums sharing the room with me. We introduced ourselves, congratulated one another on our respective new arrivals, and continued to chat until breakfast came along.

One of my room-mates, who had just brought forth her fifth, was not feeling quite as excited with life generally. As she surveyed the scene, glancing towards the big old fashioned sashcorded windows, completely bricked up outside by thick, dark, blast walls, she mumbled mournfully:-

'Looks more like bloody Parkhurst prison than the birthplace of a nation.'

We tried to cheer her up, as we laughed at her rather apt remark.

'It might be worse,' I said.

'Not much,' replied the prolific Mum. 'It's bloody purgatory till you get out of here. They won't let you go for at least ten days, and they'll make it a bloody fortnight if they can.'

'I'm in no hurry,' said I, 'I'm going to make it a holiday'.

'Some bloody holiday you'll get, my girl, they're always at you for something, if it ain't feeding yourself, it's feeding the kid or changing its nappy.'

Came the voice of experience again:-

'You're just a number here. They don't recognise you by your *face*, you know!'

During our not very elevating conversation, my Doctor was ushered into the little Ward by the Matron, his face almost hidden behind the biggest bunch of assorted Summer flowers I had ever seen — roses, scabious, carnations, dahlias and others. He pushed the colourful array into my arms, saying:-

'A selection from my garden. I like to look after the aesthetic side as well, you know!'

What a gorgeous hunk of handsome bachelor manhood, I thought.

'Thank you very very much,' I voiced, suppressing an impulse to draw him towards me for the planting of a grateful patient-to-Doctor embrace.

In spite of the doleful forecast of my unhappy room-mate, I was released from Parkhyrst on the morning of the tenth day, having had a lesson on bathing the babe before departing.

John collected me, bag and baggage, and we arrived home well before lunch. In spite of my good resolutions to stick to our former routine as far as possible, it took us all — new babe, new Papa and new Mama, several days before settling down to a NEW order of things which SHE was already dictating.

At three months old Elizabeth Ann was christened at our local Parish Church where, just over a year earlier we had tied the knot.

Quick work you may think! Perhaps, but it was pleasing to think that, anno domini permitting, both John and I would not be too ancient by the time our nipper reached her twenties.

Elizabeth's first Christmas, though quite exciting to us, did not mean very much to her. Her main fascination was the string of electric fairy lights decorating the Christmas Tree. Toys were scarce and very expensive. So a quick dive into the 'bit bag' produced many coloured wools of different thickness, which I knitted into as near a copy of our young Pooch as possible, as patchy as it was unique. We christened it George, for no special reason. And George it was who became Elizabeth's constant companion by day and by night.

While I spent my days busy with babe, baking and bargain hunting, John wasn't standing idly by. June produced a healthy crop of potatoes; cabbages like cannonballs, onions, lettuces, radishes, carrots, and peas were all presented to me during the summer months, all grown by his efforts.

Armed with pram and baby, shopping bag and as much money as I could afford to spend, I would visit the local shops several times a week. We housewives who did not go out to work were more fortunate than those who did, being at hand when anything scarce appeared in the shops. In fact we became unashamed opportunists on our shopping sprees. Often we would wait outside the grocer's or other store for ages while a lorry disgorged its load, in the hope of being first in the queue for something that had been missing from our cooking pots for a long time.

Queues formed everywhere. Often those at the tail did not know, until the news reached them, for which commodity they were waiting.

One story bandied around, almost too unlikely to be true, concerned a lady standing in a very long queue.

'What are they dishing out today?' she asked the person in front of her.

'The Tales of Hoffman,' was the quick reply.

'Never had any before. I'll join you and get some. Might make a bit of a change for dinner.'

That was only one of the tales we often heard during our shopping expeditions.

Our ration books, we were told by the Ministry of Food, were our passports for survival. They certainly did ensure fair shares of rationed commodities for all, to be supplemented daily by the availability of other goodies and the ingenuity of the housewife.

John, with a healthy appetite, was always appreciative of everything I dished up, and many times I thanked goodness he was so delightfully unfussy. Some women I met were not so lucky, and even denied themselves certain rationed or other eatables in order to please a choosy husband.

I did not really care for wartime margarine, but there were times when I would have hugged anyone who'd give me an extra half pound of the stuff.

Young Elizabeth continued to thrive. Like most adoring parents we considered her progress well in advance of other infants with whom we came in contact. At least this was the case until I happened to meet one of the ladies with babe who had shared the maternity ward with me.

Our children were just ten months old. Elizabeth, sitting up in her pram looked the very picture of good health and happiness. Her little boy, in his mother's eyes no doubt, was just as charming.

After exchanging pleasantries, she asked:-

'How're you getting on?'

'Fine thanks, and you?'

'Marvellous,' was her quick reply. 'He's even better than all my others, and they weren't at all bad.'

'So pleased to hear it,' said I, thinking MINE was every bit as wonderful as HERS.

'Can your baby walk yet?' she asked.

'No, not yet, but I'm not rushing her. Can yours?'

'Oh my goodness yes,' she replied in triumph, 'He's been walking for a couple of months,' adding, 'Can she talk yet?'

'Not much, just an odd Mummmm or Dadddd, that's all so far.'

'God bless yer, my dear, he's been jabbering away for three months, never quiet, that's him, and he can say lots of words strung together now. Has she got any teeth yet?'

'No, but I expect they'll come when they're ready.'

'He's got ten, cut his first at two months,' was her shattering remark, as she pushed open her youngster's mouth to prove it.'

I did not endeavour to count that infant's pearlies, being only too anxious to get away from the pair of them, convinced in spite of her somewhat boastful statements, that I must be the mother of a very backward child. It did not depress me, however, thinking 'Ah well, perhaps she's going to be a late developer like me.'

While on the subject of Mums and babes, an alarming incident happened around this time, concerning a premature birth in strange surroundings.

One of the Constables telephoned John to say he would be unable to peform his next tour of duty owing to a happy event at his home.

'I didn't know you were expecting one,' John told him.

'Neither did I, was the reply, adding to the air of mystery.

'Is your wife all right?' enquired John.

'Oh yes thanks, she's away for a few days staying with relatives.'

'But I thought you said a happy event — a child born, surely.'

'Yes, that's right, but it's not the WIFE.'

'A relative?' asked John.

'No. It's my next door neighbour.'

The Constable went on to explain that the young woman, in the later stages of pregnancy, had called at his home to ask him to 'phone the Midwife, as she was experiencing all the signs conducive to the impending arrival of her first-born. There was no reply to the ringing, and he had suggested the lady should sit down for a few minutes, when he would try the number again. Suddenly the lady grew pale, uttered an anxious cry, appealing, 'Whatever shall I do, I'm sure it's here.'

Three seconds later, Junior must have decided to waive professional assistance to speed his entry into this world. Before the Officer could say 'Hello stranger' the local population was increased by one.

Already trained to deal with such an emergency, the Officer went to work on the needs of mother and babe, whom he lay on the settee. He then contacted the Doctor and Midwife. They arrived shortly afterwards, attended to the two patients, and asked if 'the lodgers' might stay at the Constable's home for a couple of days, as it would be unwise to move them far at present. This he agreed to do, saying he would contact his wife who would no doubt return post haste to organise their brief stay.

As the two representatives of the Medical profession were leaving, the Doctor patted the Constable-cum-Midwife on the back, saying:- 'You've done a very good job in a tricky situation.'

'All in the course of duty,' said the hero of the day.

One morning during the late May of 1942, John came home from early duty, looking quite excited.

'Something exciting has, or is going to, happen?' I asked, recognising his mood.

'Have a guess.'

'All right then. We're on the move, promoted, or in trouble.' I hazarded.

'Not a bad effort really. Your first guess is partly true, but it's not what you imagine. No, we're not being transferred to the frozen north of the County, thank goodness. But our over-cautious superiors have at last given all officers under their wings, permission to take a holiday.'

'How marvellous. Where shall we go. I'm longing for a breath of East Coast ozone.'

'Come now, they're not all that generous, the limit is the County boundary. No straying over the border, by order!'

'Oh Lord, that cuts out nearly everywhere then.'

'Cheer up. Not quite. There are lots of lovely spots for us to explore, and I've already thought of one good place we might decide on.'

'How does Monsal Dale grab you?' asked John.

I had passed through the Dale during several outings in my 'salad days,' and the idea appealed to me.

'Anywhere will suit me as a change of scene — and our belated long overdue honeymoon.' I said enthusiastically.

'Shall I ring old Charlie up to see if his place is still functioning. You remember he retired several years ago from the Force, and bought a smallholding, and his wife runs a small Guest House.'

'What a good idea. Hope she's not fully booked.'

John duly 'phoned Charlie. After about twenty minutes of the usual Copper-to-Copper reminiscing session, they agreed a date for our week long sojourn at the Farmhouse, three weeks hence.

The looking forward time went all too slowly, and eventually the day of our departure arrived.

Ever conscious of possible impending disasters, my duty conscious husband informed me he had left our address and 'phone number at the Office in case they decided to call us back for any reason.

'I'll never forgive them if they do.' I told him, menacingly.

'Things are pretty quiet just now, so we've a sporting chance of finishing the week out,' said John, as anxious as I for a change of air.

We travelled by train, as petrol restrictions excluded the use of our car for private motoring. That ageing steam puffer's carriages could not have been more overcrowded, yet this state of affairs was typical at that time. People were standing two or three deep in every coach and corridor, sitting on each other's knees and generally squeezing up together. John and I sat on our cases most of the time, our baggage showing traces of the resultant mis-shaping and a broken lock to prove it. Elizabeth shared our knees.

At long last, and more than two hours late, we stopped at Monsal Dale Station, a tiny Halt conveniently situated in the middle of Derbyshire's hills and dales for the convenience of the few local residents or visitors to the Dale and its environs.

We emerged from the station, somewhat hot and stickily travel stained, Elizabeth being transported in her utilitarian, springless almost backless not-conducive-to-slumber-wartime pushchair. John struggled along heavily laden with two large suitcases containing all the paraphernalia necessary to see us through a week's back-to-nature, well almost, vacation.

Within eight minutes of leaving the train we arrived at the farm. The house, a large double fronted stone built structure, stood in a big garden which led right down to the river. I could not help feeling a certain amount of relief from the danger of children and water in the fact that our young lass had not yet taken the plunge of walking unaided.

Our nipper, with her friendly smile quickly scored a hit with the other residents. There were oooh's and aaah's all round.

After unpacking we joined the group of other visitors, introduced ourselves, and filed into the dining room for our first meal together — high tea.

During the meal, chatting continued, and lots of questions were asked, including:- 'Have you come far?' 'Have you been here before?' 'Have you been married long?'

'Oh dear, that last question proved to be a bit of a puzzler,' I thought, and my reply suceeded in raising one or two eyebrows.

'No, as a matter of fact we're on our honeymoon.' I said.

'Honeymoon?' asked one of the bolder of the company, as she gave an all too obvious glance at young Elizabeth.

'Well you see we were married nearly two years ago, but as John is a police officer the honeymoon had to be postponed, as were all holidays, until now.' I added, hastily, 'So I'm not a loose woman after all.'

'Better late than never — for the honeymoon, I mean,' said our doubting companion.

From conversation with our Hostess, we gathered that food was no more plentiful in her corner of the globe than it was everywhere else. Eggs from the farm were in good supply, and appeared in various forms at almost every meal. A real egg in a shell was something to which we had become unaccustomed, our eggs always turning up in dried powdery form.

The inevitable salad, lettuce-laced and pepped up with tiny helpings of cooked meat or tinned fish, popped up regularly for lunch and tea. This did not trouble our trio, as any kind of greenstuff, whether raw or cooked was among our favourite summer eats. One of the other guests, however, was not so happy at the lack of variety and originality in the meals, and moaned audibly one day:-

'We can't stand salads in any form: if we don't look like rabbits when we get home, it won't be our fault!'

There were odd times when our huge fresh air invoked appetites required a second helping of lettuce, and the hungrier, or braver, among us would ask:-

'May we have a spot more lettuce, please?'

'Certainly. Arf a mo', one of the staff would say, as she disappeared towards the garden.

A large hearty lettuce would then be pulled up, its roots whipped off with a knife, the rest of the plant being held for a brief rinse under the kitchen tap, quickly dismembered and placed into the empty bowl on the table. Thus it was not unusual for one of us to discover within its crinkly folds a caterpillar, earwig or other unwelcome creepy crawly foreign body. So ravenous were we, however, that these 'visitors' were practically ignored, or at least placed discreetly beneath a bit of spare something left on the plate.

Among our new found friends were two young married couples from Nottingham, one of whose husbands worked 'in tobacco' as she described him, and the other a grocer. During conversation on our second day together the inevitable question of the day — shortages, particularly of meat, cropped up.

George (in tobacco) remarked:-

'I've seen lots of rabbits running around here since we arrived. Wish we could take a few home with us.'

'What a good idea,' said John, 'I bet old Charlie will lend us a gun or two, or he'll know someone who will.'

'Oh dear,' said Willie, the grocer, 'I can't shoot.'

'Never mind that,' said John now full of enthusiasm, 'You just trail along with us and carry the bag and bodies.'

Charlie duly obliged, and early the following morning our valiant foot huntsmen set out on safari, having been careful to ask several local farmers' permission to shoot over their land. Our three musketeers, as we dubbed them, walked miles and miles, tracking down and shooting any unfortunate bunnies and swift-of-feet hares who happened to get within firing range. On returning to the farm, the contents of the bag were distributed among Charlie and any of his friends around at that time.

So enchanted were our male shooting trio that their game hunt became a daily occurrence. While our spouses were out tramping the countryside, we ladies spent the time walking and chatting, and entertaining young Elizabeth.

We were spared any bedtime tantrums for she had been used to going to bed not later than 7 o'clock. A similar routine was adhered to during the holiday, which left our evenings free, and there was always someone at the farm ready and willing to baby-sit for us. As our infant was already potty trained we had no problems in this direction. Although as yet plastic pants had not been invented, we had sufficient faith in her continence as to have dispensed with nappies and draw-sheet-cum-macintosh protector several weeks before leaving home.

One evening we were enjoying an after tea gossip, toying with the idea of taking a good long walk, not that either John or I needed a sleep inducer. Suddenly John said:-

'How about a brisk trek up to that hotel at the top of the hill?'

'That's The Monsal Head' said George. 'Splendid. They tell me Mine Host was quite a famous cricketer in his young days.'

'Come on, lets go then,' said John, anxious to meet a kindred sporting spirit, and off we all trooped.

We found 'Old Ship' as he was known locally, who introduced us to his wife and two charming daughters. After pleasant chat and several drinks to quench our raging thirsts, we left and took the downhill walk back to the farm, having decided to repeat the visit the next day.

On the Wednesday of our holiday, we had just returned from a pleasant walk around the Dale, when we were met at the garden gate by our Landlady. Wringing her hands, and on the brink of tears, obviously in dire distress, John enquired of her, before she had time to voice her trouble:-

'Whatever's wrong, love?'

We all sensed some serious calamity had befallen, like nothing for our tea, or could there be anything worse?

'Charlie's not back yet. He's harvesting near Bakewell, and he promised he'd be back in time for milking. Whatever shall I do. Suppose he's had an accident or a heart attack, or something. I'm all alone, and I can't milk the cows myself.'

Now John, who had had a certain amount of farm training as a lad, when he had assisted an Uncle living in his home village, had milked cows many times, though not in recent years. Without hesitation, he did his Sir Galahad act:-

'I'll do it for you,' he volunteered, to our utter amazement, for even I did not know he'd got the knack.

'I'm so grateful,' said our damsel in distress, as she wiped away her tears with the back of her hand.

'Just give me an old cap and a pail, and I'll do it straight away before we eat,' said the new 'farmhand'.

In less time than it takes to say MOO, she reappeared carrying the tools for the job. John sat down on the tiny three-legged stool and went to work. His task was made considerably easier as those ladies of the meadow proved to be the essence of good behaviour, giving not the slightest kick of disapproval at the strange hands a-squeezing of their dangling spare parts.

He milked number 1, then number 2, then 3, followed by 4 and 5, and as each pail filled up, it was replaced by another. Success, John felt, was well within his grasp. By this time, however, number 6 was getting slightly restless, annoyed perhaps by being left until the last. Alas for her, though, just as her new operative was about to begin work on her, his grip seized up completely. Every time he tried to grasp the milk squirters he just failed to get the correct pull-and-push.

Lady number 6 took a dim view of the apparent experimentation going on around her nether regions, and kicked out several times to remonstrate.

'I'll take a little rest,' said John, 'and come back later to complete the job.'

Just as he walked out of the cowshed, along came ex-Copper-cum-Farmer, Charlie, grinning from ear to ear, and no doubt wondering why everyone was crowding round his precious cows.

'Sorry I'm so late,' he apologised to his wife, whose look was a mixture of menace and relief.

'Well, you see,' he went on, 'I met old Smithy, then Jim and Arthur joined us, and who should we see just as we were splitting up but Henry from the pub, so we all went in and drank his health.'

'And so you forgot all about the time and the milking and me,' said his missus.

Charlie grinned sheepishly.

'It's no laughing matter,' said his angry spouse, 'John here has already milked five, and was going to do the last one after tea.'

'Well done,' said Charlie, patting John on the back, as he inspected the liquid result of his labours. 'I do believe you've got more out of those old gals than I usually manage. I'll buy you a pint at 'The Head' next time I see you there.'

John thanked him for the compliment to his amateur cowman.

The Friday evening we all met at 'The Head.'

'Promise me next time you come into Derbyshire you'll stay with us,' said Old Ship.

We promised.

Saturday came all too soon, and so it was back to our daily routine. Now we could begin to look forward to our next visit to 'The Head', while looking back on our first happy visit to The Dale, when Hitler refrained from cutting short our holiday — our belated honeymoon.

We sailed through the winter and spring months, and July 1943 found us fixed up for a week's holiday at 'The Head.'

As before, we travelled by train, our journey being equally uncomfortable and overcrowded. This, coupled with the fact that we had before us an uphill walk of some two miles plus to the Hotel. We alighted from the train at Great Longstone station, nerving ourselves for the trek, Elizabeth happily pushchair-borne.

The afternoon was hot and sultry. The prospect of a long walk sapped my morale. In silence we crossed the railway yard.

'Come on,' said ever energetic John, 'Let's step it out.'

Meekly I followed. We had not legged it more than a hundred yards when a car drew up with a uniform clad Police Sergeant in the driving seat.

'Hello John,' he said.

John at once recognised him as a former colleague now stationed at Tideswell, Monsal being part of his territory.

'Well, well, well,' said John, 'Fancy seeing you.'

'What a coincidence,' said I, secretly hoping he would take pity on us and offer us a lift.

'To be perfectly honest,' said the Sergeant, 'It's not exactly by chance that I'm here. You see I heard down the jolly old grapevine that you were coming to The Head for a holiday, so Old Ship and I thought I'd save your shoe leather a bit. Hop in.'

'Thanks, old man, I'll buy you a drink when we get there,' said John.

'You're too late — I've beaten you to it. I've already had one on you,' said our welcome Saint Christopher.

We were given a wonderful welcome from every member of 'Old Ship's company. We unpacked and prepared for dinner. At only two years old, Elizabeth was too young to join us for the meal. After some biscuits and a drink of milk, I took her upstairs to our huge, lofty, beautifully furnished bedroom. As I popped her into the bath, there was a light tap on the door.

'Come in,' I called.

In came dear Old Ship. Imagine my surprise when he, having toddled up the long flight of stairs, said:-

'Here's a sweetie for the nipper, and a gin and lime for you.'

'I'm sure you can do with a 'starter'. Dinner'll be ready when you come down,' he said simply.

We joined several other guests in the dining room, and exchanged brief comments across the small tables. One rather elderly couple seemed more reticent than the rest.

We were very surprised, therefore, when on our second day there, they met us on the hotel doorstep, and, with more animation than I would have guessed him capable of, the husband asked:-

'Have you seen laughing bull?'

'No, have you?' I asked, not having the faintest idea to whom or what he was referring.

'Oh yes, we've seen him every day since we came last week,' he said.

We had certainly thought them an odd pair in the dining room, but this was intriguing. We had not as yet espied any Tribal Chieftains wandering around in native costume, or anyone else who would be likely to answer such a descriptive title.

'Look, he's over there,' said the wife, pointing across a large field.

We all looked in the direction indicated.

'I can only see a cow,' said I.

'That's him, that's him,' said our lady friend, excitedly. 'That's laughing bull.'

'Now I wonder what he's got to laugh about,' asked John.

'However can a bull laugh,' I queried.

'Every time he gets a tickle at his throat,' was her reply.

'Has he got a cough then,' I asked, still unable to understand why our friend was so thrilled about a bull with a tickly throat.

'No, well not exactly,' explained our gentleman informer. 'You see they told us at the Farm that if you tickle his throat, outside, with a stick or something similar, he'll roar with laughter.'

Never having heard of a bull with a sense of humour, we could hardly wait to see this wonder of nature for ourselves. Such a phenomenon must surely not be missed, although we were very sceptical about the whole fantastic story.

Armed with a suitably long twig, we all crossed the road, stopping by the gate at the entrance to the field. Knowing the irritable nature of bulls generally, we ensured that the gate was good, strong, and securely fixed, and that His Lordship would remain on the other side.

Now that friendly specimen of bovine masculinity must have had eyesight second to none for, the moment we stopped at the gate, he tossed his woolley head into the air, and ran from the far side of the gate towards us as fast as his little short hairy legs could carry his weighty body.

'I'll try him out first,' said John, as he extended the twig in the direction of the ticklish throaty spot.

He landed right on target at the first attempt. Immediately old laughing bull opened his huge mouth so wide that I swore I could see his tonsils, (not sure whether this species have these useless addenda), and, obviously enjoying the thrilling experience, he burst into the bovine equivalent of hearty laughter, his shoulders right down to the end of his curly tail simply shaking with the thrill of it all.

We all took turns again and again, until he must have laughed himself dry of throat and hoarse. I could almost read his thoughts as he eventually scampered away, 'enough is enough!'

'When can we do it again?' asked Junior.

'We'll come after breakfast tomorrow morning, when he's got his strength up again,' John promised.

And so we were treated to at least one good, hilarious, mirthful session with L.B. each day.

'When we get back home, can we try it on old Farmer Smith's bull?' asked our infant.

'Perhaps,' I promised, but with little hope that such a rare occurrence could possibly be repeated elsewhere.

During our holiday there was never a dull moment. The weather was perfect, the company second to none, and with a laughing bull thrown in for good measure, who could have wished for more.

Old Ship took us down his deep cellar one morning.

'It's my private hide-away,' he told us, 'Gets me away from petticoat government and it'll give you a chance to cool off!'

He led all three of us down a flight of steep, roughly hewn stone steps, curved in the middle of each tread by the countless feet that must have used them since the hotel was built many many years ago. The end of our perilous descent led us to a large room whose rugged walls were further proof of its having been literally hewn out of the rugged rocks. Its main purpose, as a cool, refrigerator-like cellar for the storage of beer, wines and other commodities, was supplemented by the Landlord himself, for in one far corner of the vast expanse was a bottle of whisky and an earthenware beaker.

'None of them upstairs know of this little private 'bar' of mine,' he confided. 'But it's nice to have a little private gargle when the spirit moves me.'

Finding the atmosphere not only cold but rather creepy, and feeling sure I saw a mouse scamper away as he was talking, I decided to leave the men to their tete-a-tete and return to the surface.

John rejoined us later, saying:-

'Ship's going to lend me a gun. You don't mind if I go out for a spot of shooting, do you.'

'Not a bit — so long as I don't have to come with you. I couldn't bear to see those poor little bunnies being slaughtered by the gun.'

From then on, John disappeared early each morning, the end products being given to Old Ship to distribute among his friends.

During one of our evening strolls, which always induced the inevitable male thirst, we discovered another attractive Public House in Longstone village, The Crispin Inn.

'A good pint,' said John as he drained his first drink.

'Better than The Head?' I enquired.

'A different brew, but just as tasty.'

The Landlord and his good lady were very friendly, and charmed us with stories of the ancient Inn's history and of some of his special visitors.

The most topically exciting, and their favourite guests, were Elsie and Doris Waters, of 'Gert and Daisy' fame, who came to stay there 'to unwind' as they put it, after a busy season in showbiz.

All good things must end, and our holiday was no exception. Memories, we felt, of that unsurpassed, breathtaking view down the Dale from The Top, of laughing bull, and the general bonhomie of all we met, would never fade.

Later that year, with another week's holiday due to us, and the seaside still too far away, we availed ourselves of an opportunity to disappear for a week into the heart of the Derbyshire countryside. It came as a complete surprise from my Grandmother, who told us of a dilemma being experienced by one of her neighbours in Biggin-by-Hulland.

It was a young married couple who had recently come to live in their cottage-cum-farm-buildings-very-*small*holding place, who were anxious to visit relatives in the south of England. Their difficulty was in finding someone to feed, and generally care for, the assortment of animals they had collected during their brief residence there. Gran had mentioned John's early experience in farming, and they telephoned to ask if we could oblige. They would make no charge for our stay there if, in exchange, we would tend the livestock.

We liked the idea. John applied to Headquarters for permission to take a further seven days holiday, which was granted without argument, as they were due to him anyway.

We travelled by 'bus — three different 'buses, no less, all crowded to the running boards, the whole journey having taken more than six hours to cover a distance of around twenty miles.

We arrived just two hours after the owners had departed in their car, with three healthy thirsts and and never a Pub in sight during our two mile trek from the 'bus. That splendid couple had left the commodious pantry well stocked with all kinds of food, and a couple of crates of ale for good measure. The latter proved a great blessing, especially when we discovered the nearest hostelry was more than two miles away.

After a quick cup of tea and a refreshing wash, we surveyed the premises, inside and out, and felt sure we would be comfortable and happy.

We found the mini-menagerie consisting of two pusscats, four rabbits, several hens — black, white and khaki — and last, but by no means least, as we were soon to discover, two nanny goats.

We had no problems with any of the animals or birds, excepting those GOATS!

We had heard their anxious bleatings long before we reached the cottage on our way down the lane from the 'bus. When we saw them they were obviously not only hungry but more than ready for milking. Now John had milked a great many cows by hand in his early youth, and once quite recently at Monsal, you may recall, but GOATS NEVER.

We found a can and stool. Then, watched intently by Elizabeth and me at a safe distance, John entered the arena, or I should say, the paddock where the goats appeared to be happily grazing, minding their own business. But suddenly all that changed. Both animals looked up, eyed him very suspiciously, then pranced wildly about, backing away as he tried to capture number 1. This he finally cornered.

Cows? Easy! But Goats??? John tried all ways he could think of to coax that young four-legged beastie to 'give'. Being unused to the foibles of this particular type of mammal, it seemed he was doomed to failure before even one drop of the precious white liquid landed 'plop' inside the can. She kicked, bucked, even tried to take a piece out of his trousers, determined not to submit to a new pair of groping hands, even though its bulging bag must by now have been giving great discomfort.

If the animal was getting fed-up with the whole exercise, so was her new keeper. Eventually she struggled free. John caught her again, this time trapping her against the gate. Now escape was not possible. He had another try. But squeeze and squeeze again, still not a vestige of a trickle appeared.

'Think I'll leave them for a while and return later', said a rather disconsolate John.

In the meantime he found an old scythe in one of the buildings and proceeded to cut some grass in an adjoining field in readiness for his return to the scene of operation 'milk goat'.

Anxious to relieve the goats as soon as they decided to submit, he returned to the paddock armed with a good supply of newly mown grass. Both goats, unable to resist the prospect of a luscious grassy meal, raced towards the bearer. Oblivious to the object of the exercise, they avidly began their welcome super-scoff.

Once more, armed with the tools of his temporary employment, John stealthily approached number 1. To his great relief, she capitulated without argument. Gradually the sound of music in the form of milky trickles into the can was heard distinctly. She gave of her best, more than a pint of warm welcome liquid, not to mention her sigh of relief. Her colleague obliged likewise. Result? Almost three pints. Lovely, we thought, but when we tasted it, we were not sure of its appeal. We all decided that cow juice, on which we had been reared, was decidedly preferable to our palates. Our loss was the pussies' gain, however, as their saucers were filled up several times daily, amid loud purrings of satisfaction, telling us no doubt that we 'townies' must be ignorant to spurn such delight.

During our frequent walks around the lanes, we collected masses of hedge food in an attempt to satisfy the goats' huge appetites, while Elizabeth amused herself by picking dandelions for the bunnies.

Once tamed, the goats became quite attached to us, as we did to them, although we realised it was only 'cupboard love'. They showed their affection by nibbling at our sleeves, dresses or anything else that dangled within their reach.

We were giving the rabbit hutches a much needed spring clean one morning, when a neighbouring farmer stopped to have a word over the garden gate.

'Ow're yer gettin' on?' he enquired.

'Fine, thanks,' said John.

'It's nice for us not to 'ear they goats bleatin' their 'earts out all day and arf the neight,' he said.

'Are they as rowdy as all that?' asked John.

'Rowdy's the right word for it. It's like bloody 'Ell 'ere, and it's all cus' them townies don't gi' 'em arf enuff t'eat. Y'see they'm 'ungry beasts, allus was, and if yer dunner fill their bellies they wunner gi' yer anythin' like peace and quiet.'

'I realise that,' said John. 'That's why we spend half our time collecting stuff to keep them full and happy.'

'You'n got the reight idea. Between thee and me I canna stand they townies. They two cum from near London. They think they knows it a', but when yer gets down to brass tacks, they know nowt, leastways nowt abart country livin'!'

The cottage was very cosy, but there was just one snag, or I should say more specifically, PONG. The lounge, beautifully chintzily furnished, with marvellous views across the fields towards picturesque wooded hillsides, had been constructed on the site of an old cowshed. Consequently we could not miss the ever-present smell of cow droppings which must have saturated the foundations during countless years of bovine habitation. The strength of the odour seemed to increase during the afternoons and evenings when the sun was high and hot. For that reason we were unable to use the room, having decided that 'ashes of cow-muck' was not our favourite perfume. The living room provided a very convenient alternative, and there we relaxed when animals and birds had had their fill.

This time John took his own gun with a good supply of cartridges in case there was any chance of having a pot shot at any unsuspecting rabbit. Most of the nearby farmers gave him permission to shoot over their land at any time. One of their number, however, was not quite as amicable as the rest. He told a friend, who told another friend, who told one of my Cousins living locally:-

'It's like these townies' bloody cheek, coming here and shooting all our rabbits. They're not safe with a gun anyway, they're likely to shoot a cow or horse by mistake.'

We got the message, an overstatement to say the least, for rabbits popped up almost everywhere, and the few which John might bag could not possibly reduce the supply to any great extent, especially as true to rabbits' habits, the population was increasing all the time.

That one adverse critic did nothing to mar our enjoyment of rabbit pie, baked rabbit, stuffed rabbit, stewed rabbit, which appeared at mealtimes almost every day during our sojourn there.

'It's a wonder you didn't grow coney coats as a result,' said one of my 'townie' friends on our return home, who said she'd rather starve to death than eat rabbit in any form.

One evening, as John was leaning over the garden gate, enjoying a pipe of baccy, a young man came down the lane towards the cottage. He was quite handsome, in a dusky, brown-eyed foreign kind of way.

'Good eeeeeeveneeeeeing,' he said, in broken English.

'Hello, my friend,' said John, as the man stopped short, evidently hoping to continue the conversation.

He said he was an Italian prisoner of war, living at one of the local farms until the end of the war. Now, John who had spent some time in Northern, and later Southern, Italy, during the fighting and after the Armistice in World War 1, mentioned this to the Italian, who was very thrilled to meet someone who knew something of his native country.

We invited him indoors for a drink. He and John chatted like old pals, in fact the 'old soldiers' spent more than an hour exchanging reminiscences each of a different war. This also gave John an excellent opportunity to increase his pigeon-Italian vocabulary. The only chance he had had hitherto of airing his knowledge was at home as counter to my equally pigeon-French.

'Pass the FROMAGIO, Mum, where's the MARAMALATA, COMIS TA, BONA SIERRA? SIGNORA' just about completed his foreign language prowess.

Several visits by the Italian later just about managed to double John's linguistic capability, and although the young man came from a country with which we were at war, we decided that as some mother's son the least we could do was to give him some small bit of pleasure during his enforced stay here.

We discovered The Black Horse Inn during one of our rather lengthy walks one evening, and fell in love with its olde worlde atmosphere. We learned of its fame far and wide as providing a super pint of ale drawn straight from the wood.

We had not been there more than a few minutes before a group of young men arrived on bicycles, a cheerful bunch, simply bristling with good health and bonhomie. They parked their 'steeds' in the yard outside and entered. Soon they were all quaffing their pints and exchanging jokes — some of the drawing room quality, others to which even broadminded I turned a deaf ear.

One member of the group went straight to the piano, and before long we all joined in one of the happiest, impromptu concerts we had ever heard. Our repertoire included several popular songs of the day, including 'The White Cliffs of Dover', then to more classical hymn and song, 'Crimond', 'Rock of Ages,' and back to 'Heaven help the sailors on a night like this.'

Time went so quickly, we were all amazed when the towels were placed discreetly on the pumps, and we all took the hint and went our respective ways.

In fact the whole holiday ended all too soon. We left with happy memories of wonderful weather, reluctant goats, a happy prisoner, bunny feasts and perfect pints.

Who said 'A Policeman's Lot is Not a Happy One?' Not us.

As the wedded wife of a serving officer of the Law, I had found already that the happiest Copper is a man who has learned to relax during his leisure time, be it a few minutes, several days, or a week or two. My man had just that happy knack, a blessing which enables him, and others like him, to be ready, willing and able to cope with the arduous, trying, often exacting, sometimes exasperating job of caring for the people he is privileged to serve.

CHAPTER 6

On The Move

During the late Summer of 1943 we were approached by the owner of Manorby who told us he was considering the sale of the house, and wished to give us the first opportunity of buying it. The figure he suggested as a reasonable one to a sitting tenant was £340. It seemed to us quite a bargain, even though any day a bomb might drop in and demolish the lot.

We ventured to suggest that as the Police Authority were renting it for us, and no doubt for our successors in due course, they would expect to be approached in the first place.

In any case, it did not take many minutes to make our decision, for we just did not possess that kind of money. It would have been difficult for us at that time to find the odd £40. As we already found it impossible to save more than a few shillings a month, the balance of £300 seemed way out of our reach.

I might have been prepared to take the risk by approaching our rather austere Bank Manager. But JB had been brought up on the strict principle that any form of hire purchase, whether by weekly payments for mortgage or any other arrangement should never be indulged in. 'A millstone round your neck, to be avoided at all costs,' was his rigid opinion.

My dear old fashioned spouse, raised on the maxim that everything must be paid for before it enters the home, had no intention of bending his rule, even though as I tried quite unsuccessfully to point out, such a transaction as the purchase of the house might have ensured a roof over our heads for ever.

In our case, however, in addition to the possibility of damage by bomb, our occupation could not be guaranteed, for we were always subject, until retirement day, to being moved to anywhere in the County. If we had installed a tenant after being moved away, as John quite rationally pointed out, it might be difficult, impossible even, to obtain possession when we retired eight or more years hence.

Reluctantly I, and John with some feelings of relief, declined the offer, commonsense prevailing.

Eventually the County Council did buy the property, thus providing the permanency of a police officer's residence for as long as they wished to keep it.

Life passed by very happily, as we watched young Elizabeth develop under wartime conditions. Rationing and scarcities were still the rulers of our kitchens, dining rooms and the family exchequers, conditions which were accepted by all as the best means of providing reasonable eating, warmth and travel.

One morning during the Summer of 1944, John returned home from early duty fairly bursting with excitement. As we sat down to breakfast, he blurted out:-

'We're on the move.'

'Oh dear, where to?' I asked somewhat apprehensively, inwardly hoping our next destination was not somewhere in the frozen North of the County.

'Sandiacre, my love, just the very place I've always wanted to be in charge of. It's not often on this job that you get transferred to a place that appeals to you.'

'I'm so glad,' was my equally excited reply.

John then began to expound:-

'The boss told me this morning just before I came off duty. I shall be in charge of the whole of the Section, which includes eight villages, and we shall live at the Police Station. How about that?'

'Fine. But eight villages. Isn't that rather a tall order, even for us? But oh, just think of it, we shall have an indoor privy at last!' I said, already looking forward to a convenient convenience.

'I wouldn't bank on it,' said John, who already during his service in the Force had had considerable experience of antiquated forms of sanitation.

'When do we go?' I asked, already beginning to plan the packing.

'After seven days, that's the usual arrangement.'

'Good Heavens, we shall have to get cracking pretty quickly. I wonder if our curtains and carpets will fit. I hope there's a school nearby. Elizabeth will be starting next year, you know.'

'Now steady on, old girl,' admonished John. 'For goodness sake stop bothering about trifles. Wait till we've seen the place. I'll arrange for us to pop over tomorrow. The Sergeant there will be changing places with us here and moving into Manorby, so we can discuss our mutual plans when we meet him and his wife.'

The following morning we arrived at Sandiacre Police Station, our future home, and met the outgoing Sergeant and his wife.

In my ignorance I had always imagined a Police Station to be a purpose-built construction in a main road position, with an imposing if perhaps slightly austere outer facade. Thus I was somewhat taken aback when we found it two streets off the major road. Further disappointment followed swiftly as we came face to face with an ordinary Victorian type semi-detached villa, with old fashioned sashcord windows, slated roof, and a long narrow side yard, with blue bricks where the soil should be, and not even a window box to add a little colour to the rather dismal scene.

'Oh dear,' I thought, 'Bang go our home grown veg.'

We were escorted to the 'business end' first. This comprised the Office — a converted prison cell with a large front window facing the street, a long wooden table, a wooden four-seater form, several chairs and a cupboard.

Adjoining the Office, its counterpart in construction, was the dark unwelcoming Cell. This was a small room, the bare bricks of which were painted in two shades of darkish green. Its fixtures included a plain wooden single size bed with matching wooden pillow, a couple of neatly folded grey blankets, and a safety toilet the seat of which was firmly screwed down to the lavatory bowl. The door, a solid thick structure contained the biggest lock I had ever seen. In the door was a small hatchway through which the prisoner's food could be passed without unlocking the door. There was also a tiny peephole through which an officer could see from the outside what was happening within.

At the far end of the narrow passage leading to the house, office and cell was a small washbasin with cold water tap above. Here it was the occupant of the cell performed his ablutions.

The private living quarters were next for scrutiny. We entered by the kitchen door, which revealed a bright airy room. The equipment included an old very gnarled deep porcelain sink with equally worn wooden draining board. A Beeston boiler, set in an alcove which also housed the gas cooker, supplied domestic hot water to the house only, and central heating to the *office and cell*.

'Charming,' thought I, 'keep the prisoner and staff warm, blow the members of the household, they can sit and freeze!'

A very small but adequate understairs pantry went off one side of the kitchen. On the opposite wall was the door leading to cell and office. The living room was entered from the kitchen, and a door at the far end led to the hall, off which went stairs and lounge.

'Good God,' I remarked, 'gas lighting. That's antiquated if you like. I haven't lived with gas, except for cooking, since I was a child.'

'Yes, I'm afraid that's one of the things you'll have to get used to,' said the Sergeant's wife. It'll seem a bit dim for a day or two, but never mind. It isn't as bad as it seems. Cheer up. We're all wired up for electricity, but they say they can't come to connect us up for a long time yet, perhaps the end of the war.'

'This year, next year, some time, or.....' I laughed.

'Never,' added the lady, 'But never's a long time, so just keep hoping.'

John, who had been half listening to our conversation, having joined us from the Office, interposed:-

'I'll pop into the Electricity Offices tomorrow, and see if they can speed up the connection process a bit. It seems such a pity to be so near and yet so far from the comfort of electric lighting.'

The downstairs rooms were large and lofty, the windows big, and I wondered, visualising our smallish furniture and carpets, how we could spread it out to best advantage.

Upstairs were three spacious bedrooms, and a small oblong bathroom. I glanced around the landing, hoping to see an extra door to disclose the Loo, but failed to spy one. A Police house with no indoor toilet, and attached to a Police Station was too miserable a thought to dwell upon. Thinking I must have overlooked its presence, perhaps it was behind the bathroom door, I asked my guide:-

'Where's the toilet?'

'We've got two.'

'Two? How very convenient. Great. Indoor comfort at last. Ours is ten paces from the back door — most inconvenient, especially during air raid alerts.'

'You won't be exactly overjoyed with these when I give you their location,' she laughed.

'Where are they, then? Go on, tell me the worst.'

'Well, you see one's inside, but when I say inside, I don't mean inside the house really, because it's outside — you know, the one you saw in the Cell.'

When I had worked out that conundrum, another followed fast on its heels. Still full of hope in the case of the second Loo, I asked tentatively:-

'Where's the other, then?'

'Well now, that one's really outside,' said she, pointing toward the far end of the yard. 'It's just this side of the far boundary wall, next to the coalhouse and the stray dogs' kennel.'

'We'll be no better off than we are now at Manorby,' I thought feeling very depressed about the very thing I expected to find here.

But there was more to come, as my guide continued:-

'I always arrange it so that when I want to GO, I nip into the Cell, that is when there's no occupant there or anyone in the Office. But the trouble is you can't lock the cell door from inside, so you just sit on the 'throne' with the door ajar, hoping no-one will barge in, or come along the passage to unseat you post haste. In other words, you kind of slip into the Cell, sit, and slip out again surreptitiously, so to speak. When this doesn't work, I find it's best to trot up the yard. The trouble there is that anyone passing by in the street, or sitting in the Office, knows exactly that you're not taking a stroll up the yard for a breath of fresh air!'

'I'm curious to know the night-time procedure,' I ventured to ask.

'Well, that can be a bit complicated. You see if you go to this one during the night, you're apt to disturb any lost dog tied up there, and if he creates merry Hell during the rest of the night, the neighbours will no doubt come along in force next morning to tell you they weren't overjoyed with the concert.'

'I understand,' said I meekly, trying my best to cover up any puzzlement at having to work out the timing for every visit to one or other of the Cop Shop privies. It was not easy to imagine that when the Cell was out of bounds for one reason or another, I'd have to trek up the yard, come hail, rain or shine, gale force winds or bombs. And, whichever destination I selected, it had to be ten paces plus for relief.

'I don't know about you, but we all use the night time old fashioned Jerry. It seemed awful when we first came here, but we're quite used to it now. But there agin, you have to await your chance to empty the end product!' added my guide.

'I suppose there are worse troubles,' I said, having decided to make the best of it, when she added:-

'If it makes you feel any better, the County Authority have been talking for years about structural alterations to this property. These would include the addition of a garage up the yard, and a toilet to be made from a strip off the back bedroom. As you might expect, the war is their latest excuse for postponing the operation, so I'm afraid you're stuck with these two privies, probably to the end of your service.'

'We'll learn to live with them, I expect, for we certainly can't exist without them, can we?'

I measured up the windows for curtains. Alas, no amount of clever wartime scheming would ever make our own small casement type drapes fit large wide deep flat windows. However, a visit to my favourite Market Stall Holder would no doubt provide enough inexpensive material which I would have ample time to make up before taking over the house.

The window decor settled, we all sat down for a further chat.

'You'll be expected to man the 'phone when no officer is available — and that's pretty often,' my mentor told me.

'I shall enjoy that. Perhaps I'll be able to bring my beloved shorthand into use again.'

'You will also be expected to give personal assistance with any problems brought to the office by members of the public,' she continued. 'Then there will be stray dogs, quite often these days, who have to be fed and watered, and housed in the kennel for seven days, or until they're claimed. Most of them settle down well, thankful for somewhere to curl up snugly after days of hungrily wandering around.'

'What happens to them after your week's care?' I asked, suspecting her reply would be fateful.

'Unless somebody comes along willing to adopt them, they are taken to Ilkeston and put to sleep.'

'Oh dear, I'd just hate to see the poor little things taken away to their doom,' I said.

'Yes, I did at first, but you can't afford to be too sentimenal in this job, even though some of them do tear at your heartstrings.'

'Anything else I should know?' I enquired.

'Well, I expect you already have heard that the service YOU as a Police Officer's wife give is UNPAID, but like most of us I expect you'll do it with a cheerful countenance for the love of your old man, for the Police Section, for the County and the Country. Sometimes it pays off by paving the way to the next rung on the ladder of promotion, but generally it's just taken for granted until the time comes to retire.'

I was reminded at this juncture of something the wife of a Police Superintendent told me recently when we were discussing anyone's chances of promotion.

'Never yearn for it,' she advised, 'I used to long for George to get on, being as ambitious as the next. Yet, when it did come, where did it get me? As each higher rank was reached so our children and I saw less and less of him, until he developed into the near stranger my kids found him to be. It's a wonder they never asked, 'Mum, who's that man who sometimes calls for a quick meal and sleeps with you occasionally?'

It was time to end our visit. I must have looked a little worried.

'Don't let the move bother you. You'll soon find everything will slip into place, and you'll just love being actively busy with the lovely folk living here.'

Words of encouragement which I appreciated.

We returned to Manorby, so tiny and compact compared with our next abode.

John made arrangements with a local Removal Contractor, and packing up began in earnest.

'When packing up you must have a system,' John informed me.

He was speaking from experience gained during several house moves since he joined the Force.

Our last night at Manorby arrived at last. All was safely stored away, tea chests and cartons systematically labelled in readiness for operation unpack on the great tomorrow — our very first combined MOVE-OVER-DAY.

PART 2 : SECOND SENTENCE — 7 YEARS' HARD

CHAPTER 7

Home is the Cop-Shop — Outside Privies and All

WE ROSE at the crack of dawn on removal day. The van arrived punctually at 8.00 a.m. As usual, when an Officer was changing districts, John was given three days' leave, to enable us on Day 1 to pack up, Day 2 to depart, Day 3 to unpack and get acquainted to the new abode and surroundings.

We followed the van in our car which, from now on, would be used almost daily, although strictly for duty runs round the highways and byways of John's considerable district. Seven and a half villages would be under his wing. These included Sandiacre, our home base, part of Risley, the whole of Stanton-by-Dale including Barbadoes (remember?), Dale Abbey, Stanley Village, Stanley Common, West Hallam and Mapperley.

Sandiacre Police Section.

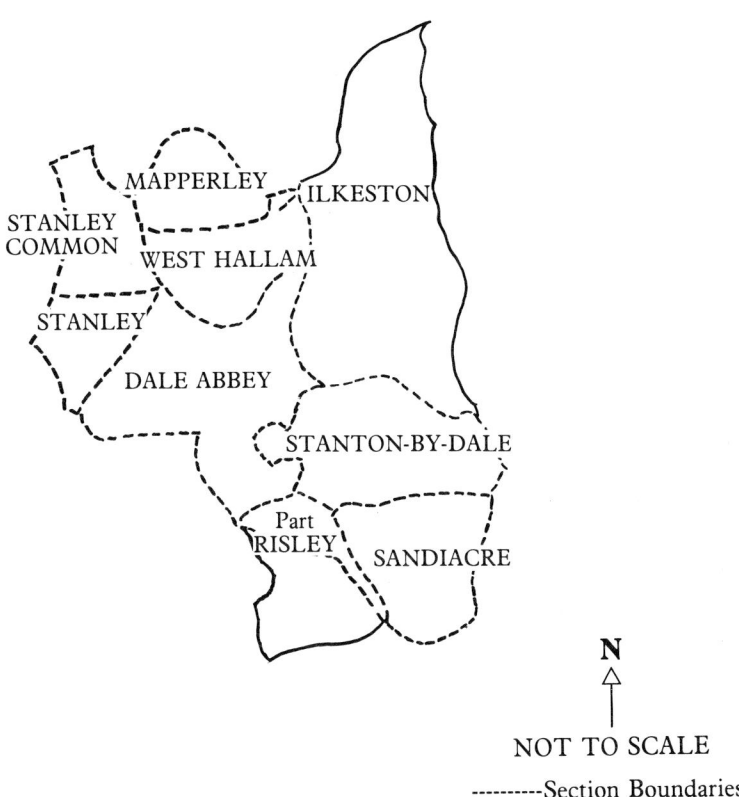

NOT TO SCALE

--------Section Boundaries.

This sketch gives a rough idea of the situation of John's territory, in relation to Ilkeston, which would still be our Divisional Headquarters.

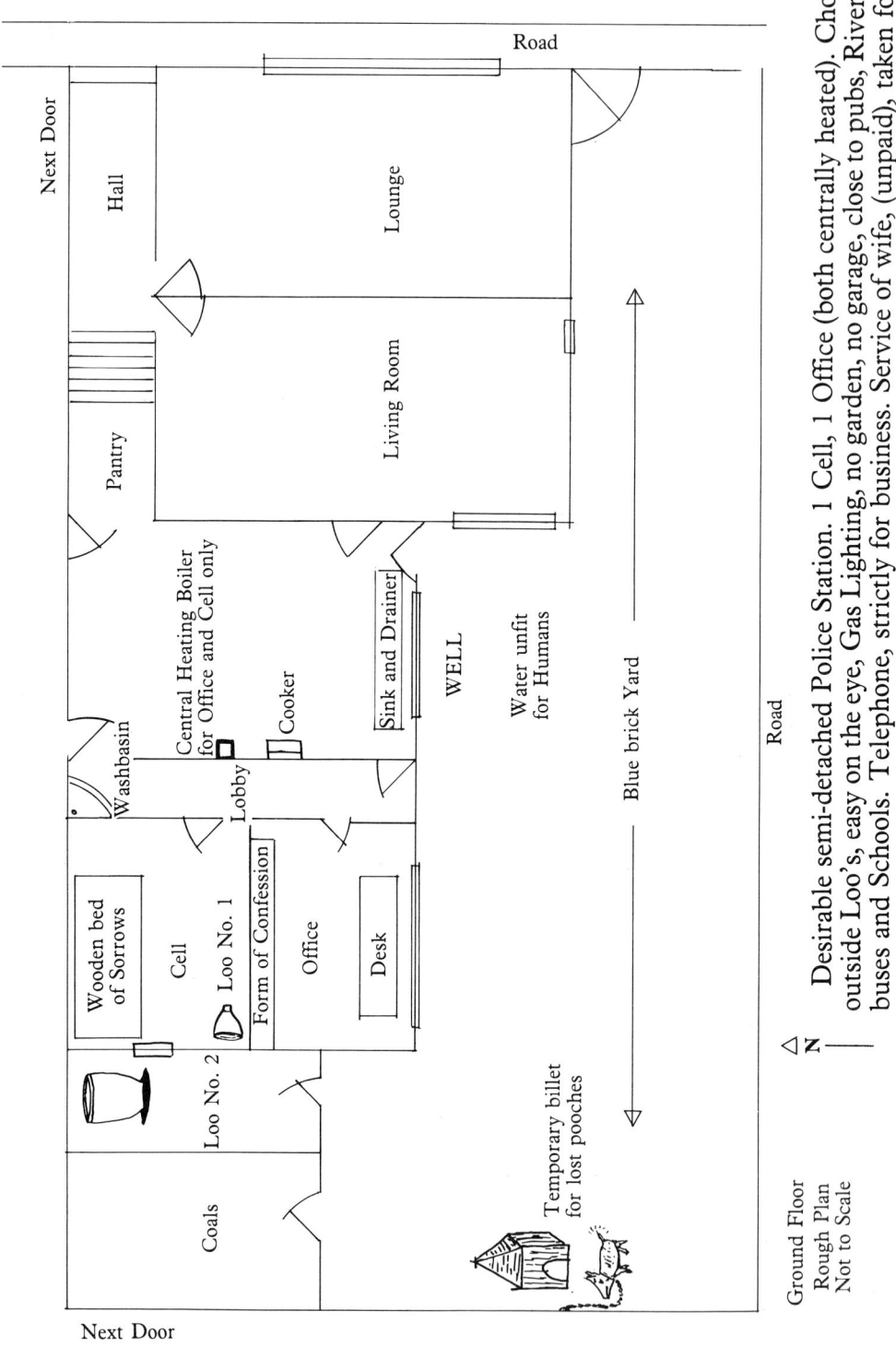

As the Police Station did not boast a garage, we were thankful, on the day of our arrival there, to be given permission to continue using the one occupied by our predecessor, situated in a Builder's yard within two minutes walk of home.

John took the opportunity shortly after the removal van had departed, to take our car round to the garage and parking it safely away until the next day.

Unpacking, mostly by my dear husband, was performed with similar regimentation as was the packing up. Everything was in its place by teatime on move-in day. This left him day number 3 to take a look round his new district and to get acquainted with the staff.

These included three locally resident serving Police Constables. Supplementing their number were three War Reserve Constables, serving in the Force for the duration of hostilities. In addition there was a Special Inspector and a number of Special Constables, whose voluntary work, performed during their leisure time proved an invaluable support to the regular officers.

Lastly, but of great importance to the efficiency of the Section were 'the girls', a thoroughly reliable, willing, cheerful group of local ladies of varying ages, numbering six in all, who also voluntarily performed evening office duties on a rota basis. Air raid alerts, or other serious events, never deterred these lasses, we were told, from turning up punctually at the office.

On my first day of unofficial duty, I met most of the staff, whom I found very friendly and anxious to help.

John spent most of his off duty time in swotting up on things rural, with the aid of general information contained in various documents and books inside his little black box, and from chatting with members of his 'team'.

'Don't overdo the study bit,' I warned him after he'd spent several hours bookworming.

'Now you mustn't get on to me. There's such a lot I've lost touch with since going to Ilkeston, and it's bound to be a bit worrying at first. I'll have to revise on the laws relating to matters agricultural, and study everything from foot-and-mouth disease to swine fever, from fowl pest to the potential ravages of the Colorado beetle, so that I don't look a perfect idiot when confronted with them.

'Carry on, Sergeant,' said I, knowing that anything I might say at this juncture would fall on stoney ground.

'Now more than ever,' continued my ever conscientious husband, 'We must do all we possibly can to keep farming going efficiently and pest free. It's one of the most vital links in our war effort. And there are umpteen farms in my villages where anything unexpected could happen these days.'

Following his patriotic outburst, I left him alone to his studies while I moved office-wards to talk to the Constable on duty.

My predecessor had already told me that the telephone must be manned by me when nobody was on duty in the office, but I did not realise until it was mentioned to me on the day of our arrival that I was not allowed to leave the house when the office was unmanned.

'Test calls are put through from HQ periodically, and you never know when they're likely to come,' said one Officer, 'And if there's no reply within ten seconds, you'll be reported for negligence, and an official ticking off will surely follow.'

'Oh dear me,' I thought, trying my best to imprint this all important instruction on my mind,

And oh dear me, it may seem incredible, but this WAS the very first thing I managed to forget!

It was a warm, sunny afternoon on our third day in the village. John was out on duty, and I decided to take young Elizabeth for a walk, combining it with a reconnoitre of the shops and to register for the supply of groceries, meat and other rationed goods.

Armed with purse, basket and small child, I carefully locked the door behind us, and with all the gay, carefree abandon of a very happy pair, we took to the main road, enjoying every minute of the exercise. I nodded and smiled and remarked on the weather to anyone we chanced to meet. The response was terrific, and I was already convinced that the inhabitants would combine to ensure our stay was successful.

'Might as well call at the Bank and get us transferred,' I said to Elizabeth as we approached the building.

We entered and I spoke to one of the Tellers, who suggested I should meet the Manager. I sat down as he disappeared into the side office.

Just as he did so, I have no idea why at that moment, but suddenly I realised that the Police Station would be completely unattended for at least another half-hour, when the duty man would make his routine once-hourly visit, lasting fifteen minutes.

Almost panic stricken at the prospect of a test call from HQ and the subsequent disgrace if the 'phone let me down, not to mention the possibility of the Superintendent, the Chief Constable even, dropping in for a call and finding no reply, I grabbed junior by the hand, dashed out into the street, never even explaining my hasty retreat to anyone in the Bank.

As we sped along homewards, I thought they would decide that Elizabeth, or I, had to pay an urgent call, and would return later. We reached home in record speed, and I sat down in the nearest chair in an effort to regain my breath and equilibrium. I realised that at this stage there was nothing I could do but wait — and hope.

I dared not mention my awful lapse to John when he came in, anxious not to add to his worries. In any case, my apparent forgetfulness would be sure to upset him.

Several days passed, shivers running up and down my spine every time I thought about my transgression. One day, hoping for a tiny spot of relief, I asked John:-

'How long would it be before I got a rocket from HQ if ever I forgot to keep the Office and house manned?'

'Is that a hypothetical question, or have you gone and dunnit?' he asked.

Not wishing to add even a little white lie to my list of sins, I confessed.

'I guessed you'd something on your mind these last few days, but you can be pretty sure if you don't hear anything within three or four days, you're in the clear. It's now nearly a week, so forget it,' he said consolingly.

I revisited the Bank the next day, and met the manager, explaining the reason for my sudden departure. We both laughed. He sympathised with me for being tied to the job. That was the beginning of a good and lasting friendship.

Cooking is one of the household chores I have always enjoyed. It dates back to the days when my Mother would allow me to lick out her cake mix bowls. Thus my weekly baking day rule was one to which I always looked forward, in spite of scarcities. Rules, however, usually have exceptions, and this one occurred on a particularly busy Friday morning.

It was always on my mind, (well, nearly always), when visiting the Loo or stuck up with dough, to be prepared to answer the telephone at top speed, even if occasionally it had meant appearing before the instrument with my pants at half-mast.

On this particular day, my thoughts miles away from possible test calls, I was just about elbow deep in plasticy dough, when the 'phone rang. Hastily I scraped off all the really loose bits, made a lightening dash to the sink to remove most of the remainder in an effort to save floor and instrument from damage by goo-ey mix, then sped into the dining room to answer the clarion call.

'Hello,' said I in my brightest voice.

There was a split second's silence. Perhaps the caller was having difficulty in getting through. Then in a moment's near panic, I feared the worst.

'You've taken exactly fourteen seconds to answer,' said the ominous deadpan voice at the other end of the line, 'You will be reported.'

I was about to explain my reason for the few seconds' delay during operation bread-to-be, when CRASH, down went the receiver, and I knew I was in dire trouble.

There seemed no point in keeping my anxiety to myself this time, as John would be bound to discover my misdeed when the 'fizzer' arrived to prove it.

When he came in from the office, I confessed:-

'I'm in telephone trouble. I took four seconds over the limit to answer, and bitchy at the other end threatened to report me. I was enveloped in dough, and only took time to give my hands a rough clean.'

'You can't blame the operator, she's only doing her job,' said John.

'That's charming,' I said, justifiably hurt I thought, 'What about me? Don't I ever get any sympathy?'

'Of course you do,' said John, realising he had put his foot in it, 'Ten seconds does seem a bit stingy to allow anyone to get to the 'phone, but rules are rules, and you'll have to try to see it doesn't happen again. But don't get too worried about it. If you are never guilty of a greater sin you'll do well.

I awaited my reprimand. The report of my transgression arrived within three days. My reasons were put in writing, and despatched to the correct quarter. By return came a right old telling off, with a warning that next time a more serious view would be taken of my carelessness. (Oh Lord, who'd be a Copper's Missus when, in an unpaid job they treat you thus?)

The Station house was just about twice the size of Manorby, and the task of keeping it clean and presentable took much longer than my periodic whips round at Manorby. Not being particularly fond of rather hum-drum, repetitive housework, I was very relieved one day on hearing of an elderly lady 'treasure', who was ready and willing to relieve me of some of my household chores. I called to see her at her home just a few doors up the street from the Station, and arranged that for the modest sum of two-shillings (10p) an hour she would assist me for three hours twice weekly. Then, having attended to my needs, she would overflow into the office and cell, payment on the same scale, the latter would be made to her by the local or County Authority.

The absence of electricity for lighting did trouble me quite a bit. I found it difficult and eystraining, to adapt to the yellow, dim gas light. I bore this inconvenience uncomplainingly for several weeks. One evening as I suffered from a severe headache, I asked John:-

'Can't you do something about the electricity?'

'Well yes, he replied, 'I'll go and see the Top Dog at the Office tomorrow. Nothing like braving the lion in his den.'

True to his word, and without making an appointment, John clad in his uniform, breezed into the Boss's sanctum on the pretext of having something of a personal nature to discuss with him.

He explained the situation.

'Glad you called in, Sarge,' said the all-powerful gentleman, 'I'm deeply sorry for the delay, but it's so hard to fit everything in these days, what with the shortage of men and materials. However, I promise you we'll attend to it tomorrow.'

'Good news,' said John, on returning home, 'You'll have proper lighting tomorrow.'

Tomorrow came, and so did the workmen. Within three hours we were in the bright lights category, (strictly behind the black-out curtains, of course).

Gradually I met the neighbours, all very friendly, if perhaps a little shy of mixing with the new Copper and his family. This slight complex did not trouble the local children, and very soon Elizabeth was happily entertaining a constant bevy of young pals and playmates.

The shopkeepers were fantastic and, although we were not guilty of breaking the law as regards actual rations, we never failed to receive a fair share of other scarce commodities, and John was always assured of a regular supply of his favourite pipe tobacco.

Sandiacre, a small busy industrial large village, or small town it could be called, was the home of a number of factories, their products including several types of engineering from gas engines, railway equipment, machine tools, also furniture, lace and other smaller items.

As regards the policing of the village itself, due to its compact nature, no Officer on duty was ever very far from the Office. In any emergency, I could quickly contact a man on the streets. Failing this, I could telephone an off-duty man at his home.

In addition to the duty men spending fifteen minutes of every hour in the office, their constant presence on the streets gave residents, young and older, every opportunity of getting to know each other. To those in trouble, an on the spot Copper could often help to relieve anxieties. To the few persistent potential criminals, most of whom our Officers knew well, the presence of an Officer walking around no doubt acted to some extent as a deterrent.

To the ordinary law abiding inhabitant, the Copper was the calm intelligent man with the friendly approach, who would nevertheless stand no 'monkey business' from anyone.

Throughout our initiation into the work of the Section, John felt only one real disappointment — the absence of a garden. One day as he was locking up the garage, the Builder-Owner of the Yard approached him with:-

'How're you settling down, Sarge?'

'Very well indeed, thanks,' said John, 'But I do miss the garden we had before we came here.'

'You can have that lot over there,' was the unexpected reply, 'That is if you don't mind hard work,' as he pointed to a large weed-ridden plot directly opposite his workshop. 'It used to grow us some real good spuds and greens, but I haven't the time these days, or the energy, to cope with it.'

John looked across to the potentially fertile spot and, ever conscious of our meagre income, coupled with his love of growing things, asked tentatively:-

'How much will it cost me?'

'Nowt,' was the quick reply, 'You can drop me off a cabbage or spud or two every now and then if you like.'

'I can't tell you how grateful I am,' said John, 'I'll start work on it this afternoon.'

He could hardly wait to tell me the good news as he came home for lunch.

'We've got ourselves a garden,' he said as he removed helmet, jacket and gloves, 'By the garage, and it won't cost us a penny in rent.'

'Our luck's really in now,' I told him, 'When are you going to start on it?'

'Well, it's in an awful neglected mess, with weeds as high as my waist. It'll take time, but it's an absolute gift.'

And so my energetic husband lost no time in going to work on nettles, thistles, twitch and many other weeds that hitherto had flourished unchecked. Often Elizabeth would accompany him on operation allotment. As he juggled with spade and fork she would spend hours sitting high up in the driving seat of a huge old steam engine of the type formerly used in Fairgrounds, parked as an out of date curio alongside the garden. A large toy indeed for a happy little girl.

In due course not a weed was in sight, and not one square foot of soil was left idle.

We frequently received callers at the office or house door reporting all kinds of things lost or mislaid. In wartime, we found the main offenders in the lost category were ration books or clothing coupons.

One morning an elderly lady knocked on the house door, saying:-

'I've lost me ration book, dearie. Has anyone found it?'

'Tell me your name and address, and I'll look among those we have in the office to see if it's there,' I told her.

She obliged. I searched, but it was not there.

'Have you any idea where you lost it?' I asked, trying to be helpful.

'Well now, duckie, I think I may have left it at the butcher's, but then again it might have been the grocer's. Oh no, I can remember picking it up off the counter, so perhaps I left it at the sweet shop, but there's a bit of a hole in the side of my bag so it may have dropped out somewhere.'

'I think the best thing you can do it to retrace your steps and ask at the likely places,' I suggested, and was on the point of telling her that if it turned up at the office we would let her know, when up piped my young Elizabeth, who evidently thought she should be in on the act.

'D'you know what my Daddy says about people who lose their ration books and things?' she asked.

'No, lovey, what does he say?'

'Well sometimes he says, 'You'll lose your head next,' and other times, he tells them to 'hang them round their bloody necks, then you'd know where to find them.'

My impulse was to give junior a sharp smack for using a swear word I didn't even know she knew, but the lady was still on the doorstep, so I postponed the treatment.

'Oh he does, does he,' said the loser, looking rather uneasy, but not quite as embarrassed as I, 'Then you can tell him from me it's the very first thing I've ever lost, so that's not too bad at eighty-five, is it?'

I gave her my sweetest smile, expressed the hope that the ration book would turn up somewhere, and admonished junior for using a word she must never say again.

The Erewash Canal flowed gently through Sandiacre, passing under a bridge on the main Nottingham-Derby road. Almost parallel with this watercourse, a few minutes walk eastwards towards Nottingham, and forming the Notts. Derbys border, was the swiftly flowing Erewash river. There was thus always plenty of controlled moisture around, which usually induced nothing more serious than a little more mist and fog during the winter months than was experienced on higher, drier terrain.

There was one occasion, completely unexpected and unwelcome, except to little boys who seem ever attracted to water in abundance when, following a

'John doing his St Christopher deed for the day'

long period of rainy days, the river overflowed its banks, flooding not only almost every cellar and the lower rooms of many houses in its wake, but covering the roads to a depth of one foot or more in places.

As ever, when trouble strikes, every member of our Police Section was called out to do their best to make life a little easier for all, whether victims in their homes, or merely wishing to cross or travel along the flooded streets.

Short of travelling by boat, and there were none in the district at the time, crossing the road was a hazardous pneumonia-inducing exercise to all who tried it the hard way by removal of socks, shoes, rolling up trouser bottoms and paddling carefully over, trying to avoid any uncovered manholes or other cavities whose covers the force of water had removed.

John and his colleagues, in between directing traffic over the flood waters, repeatedly did their Saint Christopher act by lifting bodily any woman, child, or man even, transporting them across the watery road.

One lady who availed herself of this new found means of transport, an elderly spinster living locally, told me later:-

'It wasn't 'arf a thrill for me when your cuddly husband lifted all twelve stone of me and took me safely across those swirling floods, without even a splash on my clothing. Safe in the arms of the Law at last, I thought.'

When floods and other weather hazards had disappeared, and thoughts of Spring and Summer were in everybody's minds, our local sportsmen and enthusiasts turned their attention to Cricket. They were fortunate in possessing a beautiful ground near the centre of the village. With its attractive small pavilion, ample car parking space, and plenty of ladies willing to help provide tea for players and friends, it was always a great centre of attraction.

Elizabeth and I, and John when duties allowed, spent many pleasant afternoons watching the game and chatting to the spectators. John was still a member of a Police team, and played as often as he could, bearing in mind that in his mid-forties the day must surely come when he would retire, unwillingly, from the game.

One of the highlights in the local social calendar was the Annual Show, held on the recreation ground. Here fancy dress parades were a special feature, and a huge variety of produce, handicrafts and other facets of leisure and pleasure occupations were exhibited in friendly competition.

Alas, products from our garden never managed to reach show standard, but we were always interested in seeing, and complimenting the growers of many that did.

On the afternoon before the opening of one of the Shows, I was returning by 'bus from Derby, sitting next to a young lady who lived not far from the Police station. The very first thing on which my eyes alighted, lying on the top of her basket, was the biggest cucumber I have ever seen.

'Coo, what a lovely 'cumber,' I remarked.

'Yes, isn't it a beauty,' she agreed. 'As a matter of fact, I'm putting it in the show tomorrow, and I'm sure it'll win first prize. If it does, it'll be the third year running I've won.'

'Really!' said I. 'But I thought only actual growers could compete.'

Obviously surprised at my naivity, she continued:-

'Well, officially yes, but nobody ever asks any awkward questions, and it does help to swell the number of entries. We haven't even got a garden!'

Several days after the end of the Show, that same gardener-who-never-was called across the road to me as she passed the Office:-

'I won a FIRST again with you-know-what,' beaming all over her crafty face.

I could not bring myself to congratulate her, even though apparently it was quite common practice at shows generally for non-growers to achieve similar so-called successes. What type of person, I wondered, could possibly experience such a thrill out of what I could only feel was petty dishonesty in its shabbiest form. My sympathies were with the bona fide grower who, it seemed to me, stood little chance of winning prizes against such loaded odds.

Another event, to which we as members of the Force looked forward every year, was the Annual Police Dance in one of the local schoolrooms. There, as at all similar events throughout the County, members of the Force and their friends met to trip a measure and to spend the evening in pleasant conversation, accompanied by a certain amount of liquid and more solid refreshment.

During the interval at one of our Dances, we were sitting round the 'Top Table' with the Assistant Chief Constable and his wife and a number of other members of the hierarchy. We were all chatting about nothing in particular, when a female voice from about half way down the very long table, looked the Big-Wig straight in the eye, and with a voice raised to crescendo pitch, spoke her mind, with no uncertain intent.

'Don't you think it's about time you promoted my husband? He's getting a bit tired of being just a Constable.'

A deathly hush descended upon the whole gathering, as that ambitious young woman, who had imbibed not wisely but too well, awaited his answer.

'I'll have to see what can be done about it,' replied the ACC, naturally taken aback by so bold a statement.

That lady's husband, a quiet, rather self-effacing young man, was standing nearby. He blushed visibly at the outspoken behaviour of his wife, knowing that she had just taken the very best action to damn his chances of promotion for the rest of his police service.

However, the ACC, a man well known for his understanding of human nature, must have realised it was the GIN that was giving voice. It was not very long before the Constable concerned received his three sergeants stripes, followed by two further steps up the ladder.

I guess that secretly, everyone present, and I know I was one, envied the lass for her temerity in voicing the thoughts and hopes of all those men of lower rank.

CHAPTER 8

All in the Day's Work

CRIME FIGURES in Sandiacre were no worse than in most similar places during that period. Shortages, as could be expected, induced a good deal of petty theft, the guilty ones in our Section, according to statistics, being brought to book more often than they were allowed to escape detection.

Enquiries connected with any crime were made by the Officer or Officers on duty at the time, anything of a more serious nature being passed to the Divisional Headquarters, and if necessary to County level.

At 5 o'clock one very foggy November morning, the telephone bell roused us both from our slumbers.

John, at whose bedside the extension was fixed, lifted the receiver, and still half sleepily, enquired:-

'Now then, what's up?'

'Sarge,' said the voice, 'It's Constable C here. There's been a break in at the big house on the hill. I found the back door and garage open and the car's not there. Mr. and Mrs. M are away. I've had a good look through the house, and whoever entered has vanished. Some of the rooms have been ransacked, and everything's in such a mess.'

'Where are you now?' asked John, now wide awake at the prospect of something urgently requiring his help.

'I'm in the house,' he said.

'Go into the drive,' John told him, 'And I'll meet you there in five minutes or less.'

John dressed in just about one minute flat, grabbed his nobble-headed walking stick which had so often accompanied him on similar missions, dropped his staff, otherwise truncheon, into the long narrow pocket in his trousers, and sallied forth at top speed to join the Constable, and if possible track down the intruder.

As he approached the drive he noticed a car coming up the hill travelling in the direction of Derby. Through the thick mist he just managed to discern the number plate which he recognised as belonging to one of the cars normally parked in the big house garage. He was unable to see the features of the driver, who was huddled over the steering wheel.

John realising he could not actually stop the vehicle, which was by then alongside him, did the next best thing. He threw his stick at the car, hoping it would distract the driver and cause him to stop. His aim was perfect. It hit the car and bounced off into the road.

At this juncture the Constable came running out of the drive. John shouted to him:-

'Stop that bloody car.'

Both men realised, however, this was an impossibility. Instead the Constable took a pot shot at it with his torch. It hit the side of the car which, instead of slowing down, accelerated and disappeared into the fog at a suicidal speed.

Realising no further on-the-spot action would do any good, both officers returned to base.

Shortly after their return, while still commiserating on 'the one that got away,' the telephone rang. John lifted the receiver:-

'Ilkeston HQ speaking,' said the voice, 'We've just received a report of an abandoned car in one of the lanes at the top of the hill.'

He gave the registration number, and sure enough it was the very car they had chased earlier.

Now most policemen get hunches from time to time. Sometimes they bear fruit, sometimes they do not. In this case John had the feeling that the miscreant was a local young man. On searching through the records in the office, he decided on one particular person who might be the most fitting candidate for a break in of this nature.

John already knew the fellow in question was working away somewhere, but hadn't a clue as to how to find out his address without raising any suspicions.

It was, therefore, purely coincidental that while walking round the village on the morning following the break-in, John happened to see the suspected man's Mother.

'Hello,' he said cheerfully, 'I've not seen you lately, how're you getting along?'

'Oh I'm not too bad, thanks Sarge,' she replied, 'But I'm dying for a fag and I haven't got the price of a match even.'

'If you like to come round to my place,' said Sergeant Hopeful 'I think perhaps the missus will find you one or two, though she doesn't smoke herself.'

That particular 'lamb' did not realise that she was being led well if not to the slaughter, to the 'information bureau.'

The lady's luck was in. I had an unopened packet lying in wait for such an emergency. John handed them to her. She lit up, taking the deepest of draw-ins, typical of the inveterate smoker.

'Thanks a lot, duckie,' she said, 'You've saved my life. Y'know it's at times like this that I really begin to believe you Coppers are almost human.'

'That's quite a compliment,' said John, adding by way of discreet introduction to the problem on hand:-

'How's young Y these days?'

'Oh he's doing fine. He's going straight now, you know. He's been better since he left home. He's near Brum now, working ever so hard.'

'I'm so pleased to hear it,' said John, thinking that after all his hunch might prove abortive.

'He's got lovely 'digs' too, she added, 'At No. ...... Street, ..., and happily settled down, with a new girl friend, too.'

John made a mental note of the information just imparted, saying:-

'No use, I must get on, I've got stacks of work waiting for me.'

Whereupon the lady departed, happy with her fags. John was delighted with the information she had proudly spilled out.

Contact was made with that young man who, it appeared, was suspected of other misdemeanours. He was duly apprehended and brought to Divisional HQ where he was put 'inside' — cellbound.

During question time which followed, he confessed that it had been his intention to return the car to the garage, on account of the fog. When he saw the two Officers, however, he changed his mind, knowing that he would be 'for it' if they had managed to get hold of him. He said his original intention had been to tavel to his new address with it, to add a little boast to his new-found friends.

He was duly brought before the Court and sentenced for his abortive, senseless crime.

It was not very long after this incident, after John and I had retired to bed one Saturday night, rather later than usual after entertaining several friends during the evening, that I heard the distinct sound of breaking glass. I dug his Lordship in the ribs, with:-

'I'm sure something's happened downstairs. I've just heard such a noise of smashing glass,' which was my hint for him to rise and investigate. He was not so keen.

'What the hell are you worrying about,' he said as he turned over. 'I didn't hear anything.'

He never did.

'Get off to sleep,' he admonished, 'It's only a picture fallen off the wall, so forget it.'

He was determined not to do anything about it. I was not so easily becalmed.

'Suppose someone's broken in?' I suggested.

'Who on earth would risk breaking in here, and what've we got worth pinching anyway?'

'All right then,' said I, determined to get him on his feet, 'If you won't go, I will.'

Of course this was an idle threat, for I would not have dared to leave the bedroom at that moment, just in case my fears proved real, but I did think it might bring his chivalrous instincts to work in my favour.

'All right then, if you won't settle down, I'll go and see, but you've got break-ins on your mind,' he said as, under suffrance, he disappeared downstairs.

In less than two minutes flat he was back again.

'Nothing's wrong and nobody's there,' he said triumphantly, 'So for God's sake get off to sleep and stop panicking. I've got a busy day in front of me tomorrow.'

He always had!

However, on the assumption that investigation by policeman must be reliable, I fell asleep.

Next morning, with the incident still fresh in my mind, and feeling annoyed that he considered last night's episode was merely a figment of my imagination, I set about my chores with unusually violent vim and vigour.

Having dealt with breakfast and its aftermath, I decided to give the lounge a good old tidy up after the previous night's little party.

To say that I was amazed at the spectacle before me as I opened the door would be an understatement unworthy even of me. The carpet was covered with large, medium and tiny pieces of broken glass. I looked towards the window. Three big panes were missing except for the jagged bit remaining at the sides of the frames. On various pieces of furniture were a number of pebble-like stones, one of the largest was nestling beside my best Crown Derby china tea service. It seemed a minor miracle that my cherished wedding gift had escaped damage. I looked into drawers and cupboards, and nothing appeared to have been stolen, although the stone thrower could easily have helped himself by entering through the de-glassed window.

When John came in for lunch, I was ready for him!

'Your inspection last night didn't do you justice as a Copper!' I flung at him.

I escorted him into the lounge which I had cleared of the evidence in my anxiety to forget the whole unfortunate incident. As I gave him a detailed account of the scene which met me, he merely said:-

'Now aren't you glad I didn't discover it last night. You know you wouldn't have had a wink of sleep if you'd known the windows were open to all and sundry. Go on, admit it.'

I did.

The windows were soon replaced and, purely for sentimental reasons, I decided to keep the offending stones, which I placed in a box and put in one of the bureau drawers.

Police enquiries proved abortive. The offender was never tracked down. It did hurt and worry me to think that there was somebody, probably living not far away, who thought so badly of us as to vent their spite by such petty practical proof of their dislike.

There was an amusing sequel to the stones affair several years later. Elizabeth and one of her friends were playing in the lounge one very wet day. I noticed they were extremely quiet, which was rather unusual. From experience I had found that when children's talking stops there is probably something going on worth investigating.

I peeped round the corner of the slightly open door. There I saw Elizabeth holding the 'stones box' in one hand and two of the interesting 'gems' in the other.

'Bet you've never seen anything like these before,' said my ten year old, boasting.

'No, I haven't, what are they? They's only stones, what's so special about them?' asked her playmate.

'Oh no, these aren't just any old stones. They're my Daddy's gall stones. He keeps them in this box so's he can show them to people.'

'What's gall stones, then?'

'I don't know, but I think it's something to do with his legs,' said my young progeny.' But they have to be kept secret, so you mustn't tell anyone I've shown them to you,' warned Elizabeth.

The promise was made in all seriousness.

My laughter was difficult to suppress, so I withdrew without a word, thinking it wiser to leave the two young innocents alone, rather than offer the true explanation which might have unnerved my chick. All the same, on reflection, I wondered if John might not be too keen on having his 'gall stones' flaunted before any other little girls or boys who might be enlightened one day by the two who had actually seen them, should the promise be forgotten.

Speaking of young people, we did occasionally experience a certain amount of trouble with escapees from a Boys' Remand Home situated in one of our adjacent villages.

The owner of a secondhand furniture and bric-a-brac shop in Sandiacre reported finding a brick in his shop which had shattered his large plate glass window. Among a variety of articles stolen from this smash-and-grab raid were several semi-precious rings.

Before any of our staff had time to begin their investigation, a second report of illegal entry came close on the heels of this one. An assistant from a nearby Sweets and Confectionary shop called at the office to say a window at the rear of the premises had been forced. Chocolates, sweets and cigarettes were missing.

By the usual process of elimination of suspects, John decided that possibly some of the Home Boys could have been on the rampage the night before. With a Constable he visited the Headmaster. He called in the Housemaster who had been on duty that night.

This particular Housemaster had previously been of great assistance with similar spots of bother in the recent past. He was given details of the two incidents.

'Leave it to me, Sarge,' he said, 'And I'll contact you later. If it's any of our young blighters, I'll ferret them out.'

Whereupon the Officers departed, their souls full of hope.

Sure enough, and true to his word, the 'phone rang next day.

'Can you come up,' asked the Housemaster, 'I've some good news for you.'

At once John revisited the Home.

The Master explained how he had lain in wait the previous night, just in case the boys, emboldened by their previous escapade, might have been tempted to repeat the safari.

When he had given all the boys the impression that he was going to bed he had remained instead in his unlit office. It was not very long before he saw several boys creeping surreptitiously across the lawn. He followed, and finally caught up with them.

'It didn't take very long for them to confess everything, Sarge,' he said, proving it by showing John most of the missing property, with the exception of some sweets and cigarettes the boys had already consumed, or distributed among their friends.

'Two more crimes solved,' said John. 'Praise be for the statistics.'

In fact so perfect was the entire investigation that the owner of the secondhand shop said they had returned more rings and other small articles than he had missed!

The pre-Christmas period was always one during which extra Police vigilance was essential. Although it is almost impossible to catch a housebreaker in the act of doing his worst, time can often be saved in tracking him down by a quick response on the part of the investigating officer.

A telephoned report from a gentleman living in a house on the outskirts of Sandiacre, told us that he and his wife had just returned home from doing some of their Christmas shopping, to find everything in an absolute mess.

Every cupboard and drawer in the house had been ransacked, and the bedding and beds thrown about. The Christmas cake, iced only the previous day had been smashed against a wall. A bottle, filled with sixpenny pieces saved for a charity had gone, although the thief, in his haste to decamp, had spilled a number of them over the carpet. Other articles missing included ornaments, jewellery, cash and many other small items. A large new suitcase had also been taken, no doubt packed by the intruder with the swag.

We learned some time later that this particular thief had left a trail of similar break-ins over more than a forty mile area. He was apprehended, and charged with the Sandiacre offence along with all the rest. He was 'sent down' for a lengthy period.

I shall never forget the distress suffered by that lady, as she described her horror at the spectacle confronting her on entering the house, after a happy shopping expedition in town.

Several months after her experience, I met her one day in the village.

'I just can't forget it,' she said. 'That horrific incident is printed indelibly on my mind. Do you know, every time I turn the key in the door, after going out, I tremble and feel sick with the thought of it all.'

I often wonder if thieves ever stop for one moment to think of the awful reaction suffered by their victims. How would they feel if the positions were reversed?

We seldom received a report of a break-in which resulted in nothing having been stolen. This did happen once, when the Managing Director of a local company 'phoned early one morning to say that the works Canteen had been entered during the night.

'Anything missing?' I asked.

'No, nothing as far as I've been able to check. Please tell the Sergeant to come over. He'll have to see to believe the damage they've done.'

Accompanied by a Constable, John went at once to the scene of the crime.

Everything from floor to ceiling in that beautifully appointed Canteen had been bespattered with the contents of various sauce bottles. It lay in pools on tables, chairs and the floor. It dripped from the walls, was plastered down the doors. When the supply of sauce had been finally exhausted, extra liquid in the way of urine had been generously splashed around.

When John explained the chaos to me, I felt disgusted that any human being could be so idiotic as to behave in such a manner.

'Surely it must be the work of a group of kids,' I suggested.

'You're probably right,' said John.

Enquiries later led our Officers to a small group of young boys, who at first denied they had ever been near the place. Eventually they confessed, excusing their unusual behaviour with:-

'We didn't have anything to do. We were bored, so we thought we'd have a bit of fun.'

That bit of fun let them all through the usual channels of reprimand, with stern warning in Court never to repeat such a ridiculous performance.

'Satan finds work for idle hands to do was never truer than in this case,' I told the two Officers as they returned from Court.

Most of the people in Sandiacre and the rest of our extensive district lived normal lives with normal minds. Kinky crimes seldom came to our notice. One in particular comes to mind.

It concerned a number of articles of ladies' lingerie reported missing from several local clothes lines.

Enquiries led the Officers to a young man who at first denied all knowledge of the offences. Persistence by the arm of the Law was rewarded in due course, however, when the man broke down.

'If I do tell you it was me, you won't say anything to the wife, will you? She'll kill me if you do.'

Naturally John could not make such a promise. The man, having confessed so far could not very well deny his involvement any longer, even though his wife might find it difficult to understand, or excuse, this peculiar foible of her man.

He explained his inveterate titillation when feeling anything of a silky texture, producing several of the missing garments from beneath his pillow and other hiding places in the house.

That particular knicker-nicker was duly hauled up before the Court, and psychiatric treatment recommended. In the meantime he was strongly advised to keep his odd behaviour strictly within the four walls of his home, or preferably to indulge himself with some anti-titillatory habit.

The local children very rarely gave us any trouble. There was one small boy, however, guilty of petty theft, for whom my strict disciplinarian husband felt sorry.

It was during enquiries regarding a number of instances of petty thieving that John's enquiries led him to a lad of eleven years. As always in such circumstances, the boy's Father was present during the police interrogation.

After trying, rather unsuccessfully to lie his way out of it, the boy brought forth a full confession. His father was absolutely livid. At once he picked up the first implement of torture that happened to be at hand — the boy's cricket bat — and, in John's presence, that lad's Dad gave him the biggest good hiding on his bottom that, short of damaging the boy's spine, John ever hoped to witness.

The beating at last over, Dad spoke first. Breathless from the effort, and the lad streaming with tears, he said:-

'I believe in tackling this sort of problem on the spot. There's nothing more effective than a good belting to make him see sense. My own Dad used it on me. It worked then, and it's bloody well going to work now. You can take it from me, there won't be any more bother with this kid of mine.'

Several years later, John met the lad again, now adult, smartly dressed, very polite. Recalling his earlier bashing by his father, which he said he would never forget, he told John:-

'Best day's work my Dad ever did. I realised then that crime doesn't pay.'

Another unexpected incident, quite different from the last, concerned a knock at the house door just as John and I were having our bedtime cocoa and biscuits.

'What's to do now?' I asked John, as he donned his uniform.

'Nothing much. A man on a motor-bike has fallen into the Canal. He's swum to the other side and is making for Nottingham. We're going to try to catch him. Wait up till I come back. I may need your help. In any case, he'll want some dry clothes.'

I waited. Twenty minutes later I heard footsteps in the yard. Looking out of the window I saw their saturated victim being led dripping into the office. John entered the kitchen.

'Fetch me a bath towel and one of my old vests, and that old pair of gardening trousers and worn jacket. Poor devil's wet through.'

I did as I was ordered, collected the garments and took them to the office, together with a big mug of hot steaming sweet tea.

There before me was a woebegone, dejected, shivering young man. He was telling the Officers he was a University Student studying for the Ministry, and was on his way to Nottingham to visit relatives. In the blackness of the night he had lost his bearings, had turned left at the canal bridge traffic lights too sharply, and plunged into the dark, deep waters of the canal, bike and all.

'Can't stop long here,' he added, 'My relations are expecting me.'

'You cannot leave here until your clothes are dry, and that will take some hours.' John told him in no uncertain terms.

Although the young man's story seemed quite plausible, John felt it did not quite ring true. After extensive enquiries made to other Forces and Institutions, the name and address of his Nottingham relatives came to light.

They were contacted, and came to the Office to collect the unwilling swimmer.

John's doubt as to the authenticity of his story proved true. He had escaped from a Mental Institution, with the sole intention of gaining his freedom. He had no ciminal record.

The motor cycle was recovered from its watery grave, and returned to its rightful owner, having been 'borrowed' by the young man to speed his getaway.

Among the Magistrates sitting at Ilkeston was one highly respected gentleman well known in our district. He happened to be on the bench when a young soldier was charged with exposing himself by somewhat proudly showing off his 'credentials' to a young lady living near the outskirts of Sandiacre.

Unfortunately for the man in question, the incident happened as a local Builder was passing in his car. He reported it to the Office. At once John jumped into the car and sped towards the scene of the crime.

During his description of the soldier, our Builder friend mentioned that his uniform tunic had a red shoulder flash, the most conspicuous feature of his dress.

As he was approaching the place where the offence occurred, John noticed a soldier entering a nearby shop, a red flash showing up brightly in the sunshine.

There are times when a Copper is on to a suspect that he has to take a risk. This was one of those occasions. Without stopping to consider that there might perhaps be other quite innocent local soldiers around with red flashes, John approached him.

'Get into this car,' John ordered him in no uncertain terms.

Whether the look of surprise on the man's face was one of guilt and apprehension John neither knew nor cared at that moment.

They arrived in the Office. At first, as is usual in such cases, he denied the offence. The brief interrogation ended when he finally capitulated.

His excuse, the most popular one in cases of this type, was that he had never done anything like it before, and he could not explain his sudden urge.

He appeared before the Court. His Commanding Officer entered the witness box, and extolled all the man's virtues, including his devotion to duty, complete honesty and moral uprightness. The act, in his opinion, was completely out of character.

'I recommend a course of psychiatry,' said the Superior Officer, 'There's nothing wrong with this man that this kind of treatment will not cure.'

Now that particular Magistrate, a man of great integrity, renowned for his understanding of the problems of people in all kinds of trouble, was known locally as 'one of the old school,' a firm believer in the deterrent effect of making the punishment fit the crime.

'Psychiatry, psychiatry,' he repeated, 'MMMMMM, Yes, now let me see. That's this new-fangled stuff, isn't it?'

'Yes, Your Lordship,' said the C.O., so obviously confident of the success of his plea on behalf of the soldier.

Then, with half closed eyes, and peering over the top of his metal rimmed spectacles perched somewhat perilously on the end of his nose, the magistrate added:-

'Well, No. I think this time we'll give him a bit of the OLD — SIX MONTHS!!'

A hush descended on the Courtroom, the prisoner was taken down, (with trousers well buttoned up) on his way to serve his remedial sentence, based on that Magistrate's practical recipe for future good moral behaviour.

'He should have given him twelve,' I told John when he returned.

'Six months should lick him into shape,' said John. 'And I agree with the magistrate that if psychiatric treatment became general practice for similar or worse sexual offences, the women would be in far greater danger than they are at present, war and all.'

In those days we hardly ever saw a man or woman the worse for drink. We received a message one Saturday afternoon from a woman who said her daughter's husband had arrived home hopelessly and helplessly drunk, and showing violence towards his wife. Before going round to investigate, John telephoned one of the local Doctors, who came to the office at once, accompanied by one of his Partners.

As they arrived, I noticed young Elizabeth dashed out of the room and flew upstairs. John and the two medics departed to see what they could do about the inebriate.

I called to Elizabeth, but received no reply. Thinking she was happily occupied in her bedroom, I left her. Half-an-hour later, I heard a frightened little voice saying:-

'Has that big drunk gone away yet?'

'Which drunk?' I asked. 'Whatever gave you the idea those two men were drunk. They were both Doctors.'

'Oh dear,' said a relieved young lady, 'When I heard the Constable telling you about a drunken man, I thought the big one was rolling about a bit.'

'Your imagination, my dear. If he had been you're always quite safe when Daddy's around, and so am I. The Doctors had come to go round with him to the man's house just in case he needed a tablet or something to make him sober again.'

Thus reassured, the incident was never mentioned again, and was soon forgotten. I suppose, like me from the days of my early youth's experience with my Father, Elizabeth had an instinctive fear of all who reeled about as the result of over-imbibing.

Although we had the use of the Cell for our own convenience when convenient, it was always available to house any 'lodger' deemed safer under lock and key. It was very seldom that any wrong doer was forced to take advantage of our 'hospitality.' This was partly due to the fact that people in those days just did not have the money to spend on such luxuries, and perhaps the wartime beverage did not quite come up to former strength, but largely because most suspects were taken direct to Ilkeston, where ample accommodation of a similar kind was always available.

There was one noisy night, however, that I spent when a well and truly intoxicated man had to be incarcerated in our Cell, largely for his own safety's sake.

One Saturday night, as John and a Constable were standing on the Market Place, as was their custom just as the Pubs were closing down for the night, they were approached by a man who reeled and rolled around.

'I want to be locked up,' he told the astonished Coppers.

'Where are you from?' asked John.

'Bloody Beeston, and I don't want to go back there, not tonight, no thank you, my missus will murder me.'

John and his colleague had other ideas, however. They stopped the next 'bus, intending to send the man on his way. There was a slight scuffle. The man went completely limp, refusing to leave or even get up from the pavement where he was lying.

The 'bus driver and conductor were getting worried, as waiting time was up.

'No use, Sarge,' said the conductor, 'We'll have to go, or we'll be in trouble if we're late.

The vehicle moved off without their unwilling passenger. The man sat up but refused to move. Both Officers walked away, and returned to the Office. They spent the usual fifteen minutes inside, and had just locked the door when who should meet them outside? His drunken lordship!

'Go on, do me a favour, lock me up,' he pleaded.

'Right,' said JB as he grabbed him by the scruff of the neck. 'You're in.'

He was duly consigned to the Cell, obviously delighted to have got his own way, safe from his spouse's scorn and torment.

He was given two blankets, thrust on to the wooden bed, told to be very quiet and get off to sleep.

On that particular night I was sleeping in the back bedroom, directly over the Cell, as we were in process of redecorating our usual sleeping quarters.

Suddenly I was aroused by the loudest moans and groans it had ever been my misfortune to hear, coming from underneath my bed, or so it seemed. This was followed by a falsetto voice shouting to the Good Lord to preserve him, with the addition of a string of invectives which only a drunk could spit out.

'There must be someone inside,' I thought.

I went downstairs to investigate. I did not feel too scared, as I knew that if the cell was occupied there would be an Officer on duty in the office throughout the night.

I listened outside the Cell. He was in there all right, and repeating the dreadful language I had already heard upstairs. I had decided to return to bed when John entered the kitchen. He assured me there was nothing to worry about.

'It's only a rather rowdy drunk,' he explained. 'I'm just going to 'phone his wife to ask her to arrange to collect him so he probably won't be here very long.' Wait a minute or two and I'll tell you what transpired.'

John reappeared.

'I told his wife her husband is here, the worse for drink, and she would be well advised to arrange for his release.' said John. 'You'll never guess what she said.'

'Go on, tell me she's not interested.'

'You're almost correct. She said 'I'm not sending for that bugger. I've had a-bloody-nuff of him, he can bloody well stay there till he's sobered up, and then I'll decide what to do with him.'

'So we've got a lodger, willy-nilly, have we?'

As I returned to my lonely bed, silence reigned. But not for long. The swearing began again. I tried not to listen. Then I heard the stentorian tones of the duty Constable, saying:-

'Get on that bed, will you, and shut up for Christ's sake. You've already wakened all the household. Get up off the floor, and take your head out of the lavatory,' said the Constable.

'Leave me alone, leave me alone. Don't thump me, will you,' said the drunk.

'You needn't worry, I won't thump you, we never do, but I'm not saying that you're not asking for the treatment,' said the Officer, no doubt as fed-up with the man as I was.

Alone once more, the railings of the inmate continued, this time appealing to the Almighty for deliverance. From what? I wondered — his Missus, perhaps.

I managed to snatch some sleep, and was relieved when morning came at last. I had left the Officer a spot of supper, a roll-mop herring and home-made cob, as was my custom when I had had a baking session.

I rose at about the usual time, and as I crossed the hall, I noticed a small slip of paper lying underneath the letterbox. It read:-

> In prison cell as drunken lout
> Appeals to Christ to let him out,
> I sit alone and long to tell
> That rowdy sod to go to Hell.
> Instead, I'll eat your supper dish
> Of home-made cob and roll-mop fish.
> Oh Mrs. B. I think you're grand,
> The best Cop's wife in all the land!

A Copper bursting into rhyme? Unusual and very charming, and flattering. I did appreciate too the sincerity of the odd ode.

Breakfast, offered to our noisy 'lodger', now full of alcoholic remorse, was flatly refused. Having spent a drunken night leaning up against and over the cold toilet, it was not surprising that he could not face the thought, let alone the sight of food.

John bailed him to appear in Court. As the man was about to leave the office, the Constable suggested he should apologise to me for keeping me and my six children awake all night to the tune of his ramblings.

He knocked on the kitchen door. With cap in hand, and looking pathetically foolish and penitent, he said.-

'Sorry, lady, sorry I made a bit of a din last night, keeping all your six kids awake. Won't do it again, I promise.'

'That's all right this time,' I told him and, putting on my sternest expression and voice, 'I don't want to see you here ever again.'

'My word, you won't. I've made up my mind. I'll never touch another drop of the stuff again.'

A resolution I felt certain he would not keep for more than a couple of days. My own Father regularly made such a vow, but broke it the next time he met 'the boys.'

I admired his resolution, but doubted its permanence, and laughed inwardly at the thought that my family had grown so large overnight!

Crime occupied some of the Officers' time, though fortunately not too often. Accidents on the roads also happened from time to time, particularly along the main roads.

One night, we were cosily tucked up in bed, fast asleep, at peace with the world, when an unusually loud crash, followed by a series of bumps and the smashing of glass, disturbed me from my slumbers. JB, as usual, did not move a muscle, until I gave him a dig in the ribs.

'What the Hell's going off?' he asked, considerably irritated by my prods.

'That's what I'd like to know,' said I, describing the terrible din I had heard.

'Get off to sleep, you've been dreaming again,' was all I received by way of reply.

'I haven't, you know, not this time,' I persisted.

Just as JB was in the act of turning over to complete his quota of sleep, a loud knock on the front door seemed to indicate that what I heard a few minutes earlier was no reverie.

'John leapt out of bed, threw open the window where, underneath was a very worried night duty Constable.

'Come quickly, Sarge,' said the voice, 'There's been a nasty accident at the traffic lights. In fact they've nearly been wrecked, and the control box on the bridge has been moved.'

'Go back there at once, and stand a safe distance from the box and don't move till I come,' said Sarge.

'You were right this time, old dear,' he admitted, 'Trouble at the traffic lights. Perhaps it's a blessing in disguise, for they're always going wrong. We'll get a new set now, maybe,' he said as he disappeared downstairs and into the night.

Sleep forsook me for the rest of the night. John returned as dawn broke.

'Whatever was it,' I enquired.

'An Army lorry out of control, and by a near miracle the driver suffered only superficial scratches. Apparently as he was approaching the lights his brakes refused to work, so he steered the lorry as well as he could, hitting the nearside lighting column, which he uprooted. He then careered across the road, tackled the Canal bridge sideways on, and crashed into the control box which he completely dislodged.'

'That could be a bit dangerous, couldn't it?'

'A bit? You're joking. That live cable standing up in the middle of the pavement could be lethal to anyone passing by at too close quarters. I've 'phoned the engineers who are coming at once to make it safe, but there won't be any lights for some time. One of us will have to direct the traffic instead.'

'Another job for the boys. Ah well, variety is the spice of life, we're told,' was my comment, which was met by JB with a snigger.

'I've never seen so much broken glass everywhere,' said John, but some men will clear it up as soon as possible.'

In due course, after many traffic controlling sessions by Sarge and his men, we were treated to a brand new set of traffic lights.

'It's an ill wind......' I remarked as I witnessed the very first switch on.

'It certainly was a bit of luck from our point of view,' agreed a Constable standing by my side.

Family squabbles, during our sojourn in Sandiacre, were very few and far between. At least those to reach our ears were rare. Break-ups between man and wife, spouse bashing, or similar domestic strife seldom came our way.

There was one occasion when a local shopkeeper ran round to the office at midnight, asking for protection from his wife in her fury. She had threatened him with the sharp end of the carving knife when he arrived home well 'oiled'.

'She's put the knife under her pillow, Sarge, and I don't mind telling you, when she's in this mood, anything can happen. She's good enough to wait till I'm asleep and plunge it into my heart, then you'll have something really nasty on your hands.'

John, who knew both parties well, suggested that a little tactful persuasion on his part might help the situation. He accompanied the husband towards home and a reconciliation, and the return of the implement of torture to the kitchen drawer.

They entered the house by the back door. They tried the bedroom door. It was locked on the inside.

'Leave this to me,' whispered John.

'This is Sergeant Broughton,' he said, addressing the locked-in lady, 'May I have a quiet word with you, please?'

'I'm not letting that devil in here no matter what you say, or what he's told you making his side right,' was her immediate reply.

'Now, now, be a good lass, put on your dressing gown and come downstairs. I'm sure between us we can iron out your troubles,' said John in his most persuasive tone.

'O.K. Sarge, I'll do it for you, but not for him, understand?'

Husband and John retreated down the stairs, followed several minutes later by a slightly calmer wife.

'What's all this I hear about you threatening your hubby with a knife,' asked JB. 'I thought the war was against Hitler.'

'I only did it to scare him. You've no idea what I've had to put up with from him over the years. I've just about had as much as I can take,' she said, in an endeavour to put her side of the argument.

At this point her husband intervened.

'Come on now, get it over quickly, and let's be friends again. You know I've to be up at 4.30 in the morning. I'm sorry, but you know what it's like when I run into the lads at the Club.'

'I certainly do know, but I'm not sure if the LADS weren't women, to keep up your sexy reputation,' she retorted.

'Now look here you two,' said Sarge, as anxious as he was to retire for the night, 'Why not kiss and make up, or at any rate call a truce until the morning.'

Husband and wife looked at each other. All three present began to laugh. Peace reigned once more.

'Have a wee droppie before you go,' suggested the lady to John.

'I'm still on duty, my dear, so no thanks. I'll pop in some other time though,' replied honest John.

Turning to her husband she said:-

'You're not going to get one, you don't deserve it.'

John thought the time was right to leave, but before doing so he said:-

'Run upstairs, there's a good lass, and fetch that knife. I want to see it safely back in the kitchen drawer where it belongs. And promise me you won't do anything so foolish again. There's much better and safer ways of settling an argument.'

'God knows I'll try, but it sometimes takes a superhuman effort,' she promised.

I never discovered whether there was a full moon on that particular night, but when John returned to the Office another shopkeeper was awaiting him.

'I want protection,' he told John, clutching his arm as he tried to get the key into the office door lock.

'Come in then. Protection from what?'

'It isn't WHAT IT'S WHO,' said the man.

'Who then?' queried John.

'It's the wife. She's gone berserk, and is threatening me with all sorts of terrible things, and I'm afraid she'll do me in.'

'We'd better go along to your place and try to sort you out,' suggested JB.

They entered the kitchen and found the wife sitting, sipping from a glass of water, or might have been Gin.

'Now then,' said John, 'What's the trouble between you?'

'Trouble?' she replied, 'Trouble, there's no trouble, we've just had a friendly argument. He always makes it out to be far worse than it is. It was just one of our tired tiffs, you know, after we've been busy in the shop all day. I admit I do go off the deep end sometimes, but it's me Celtic blood. I get so angry I just let fly at whoever's around, and it usually happens to be him,' she said, pointing at her victim.

'Well then, perhaps in future you'll try to keep your rows and threats right here. We don't want to be involved in any of your so-called 'friendly' arguments. If ever you do anything really serious, then you, intelligent folk that you are, must know the consequences. Now get off to bed, both of you, and let's have no more of it,' said John as he closed the door behind him.

John called on them the next day to ensure that all was well. The lady confided that they both had to take sleeping tablets to get off to sleep, and sometimes they were more than just dozey before they reached the top of the stairs.

I suppose, being in the drug business they had access to this or any other type of medication, but it struck me that to start the habit at their age was both foolish and unnecessary.

As John and I believed sincerely in leaving all kinds of tablets on the Chemists' shelves, I thanked my creator that so far at least he and I had been fortunate in avoiding any such habit forming panaceas.

Was the moon responsible for the night's excitements?

He had just entered the hall on his way to a belated sleep, when an urgent rat-a-tat-tat on the front door revealed a man who appeared more than usually agitated. Standing at his side was a woman with a child.

'I've just picked up this lady and her daughter in my lorry on Derby Road. She says her husband's locked her out and he's got a gun and is threatening them with it.'

'You'd better come into the office, then,' suggested John.

They all entered. The woman and girl were shivering from heads to feet, dressed only in their night attire on a cold, frosty night.

The lorry driver took his leave, having been thanked by both his passengers and by John for bringing them down.

Between her sobs and shivers the woman related the whole story. Apparently her husband had been drinking and was not really responsible for his actions.

In such a situation it would have been folly to suggest their return home. They mentioned a relative who lived in the village who would probably agree to give them shelter at least until the next day. Contact was made by John by 'phone, and arrangements made for him to transport them forthwith to their welcome haven.

John visited the gunman, a mild friendly soul in normal circumstances. As so often happens after a drinking bout, he was full of remorse for something about which he could remember absolutely nothing. A reunion with the family followed, and a promise never to repeat the threat again given, though for how long it would last was open to conjecture.

CHAPTER 9

H.P., A Ghost, and a Graveyard Safari

OUR FINANCES, always extremely tight since we were wed, had not allowed us to indulge in any of the modern labour saving gadgets or furniture available at the time. There were odd times when I did long for various items of such equipment, but never felt desperately deprived. At least not until after Close Down one General Election Day, when the Returning Officer and his wife called in at the office.

While he and John were enshrined in the inner sanctum discussing the excitement of the Big Day in British Politics, she sat with me in the house.

During our conversation on generalities, such as the state of the national economy and the weather, we turned to things domestic.

'I should be absolutely lost and tired out if I didn't have my 'fridge, vacuum cleaner and washer,' she told me. 'Of course we've bought our own house, and it's brim full of all the latest mod. cons.'

I did not enlighten her as to my lack of such luxuries, but when she finally departed I could not help thinking:-

'Oh dear, I'll never be able to afford a 'fridge, vac. or washer, and as to buying a house for our retirement that was the most unlikely of hopes and expectations.

Yes, I don't deny it, I was rather more than a teeny weeny bit envious of that fortunate lady, whose husband's apparent success financially had enabled them to live their labour-saving lives.

I awoke the next morning feeling rather unusually depressed. But this mood is not really ME. It was a lovely sunny morning, so as part of the cheering up process, I boarded a 'bus to Long Eaton, some two miles distant, intending to treat myself to a spot of therapy in the form of shop gazing — strictly from the outside, with neither the money nor the intention for anything more.

During my pavement plodding I saw fine examples of all the things the good lady had told me about the evening before.

'Perhaps when His Nibs retired,' I consoled myself, 'We'll be able to obtain some of them, at least.'

That seemed so far ahead, pie in the sky, and by then we'd perhaps be too old to care.

'Think,' I mused, 'When he leaves the stick-to-the-rules old Force, I'll be able to get a job, and the extra money is bound to help.'

Just at that moment, my eyes alighted on a window displaying all kinds of kitchen equipment, marked with tickets stating ...so much per week, with no sign of the full price.

Short of a minor brainstorm, I do not know to this day what possessed me, but on impulse I entered the shop, 'only to have a closer look' I told myself.

The shop assistant suddenly appeared from the rear of the showroom.

'Good day, Madam,' he said in dulcet tones, 'Can I help you?'

'No thanks,' was my hasty reply, intended to put him off, 'I'm only taking a quick look round.'

'Everything's at knock-down prices, and can never be repeated. It'll pay to buy now, I can assure you.'

'I rather like that kitchen cabinet over there, the tall blue one with pretty glass upper doors,' I ventured to say.

'Now that's really the bargain of the week,' he said, 'Just think, no deposit and only 1/9d. a week. I'm sure you could easily manage that luv.'

'Oh, I don't know, you see my husband is very much anti HP.'

'But think how it would enhance your kitchen,' said the persuasive one.

And, before I could think of any further arguments against it, I had signed a document promising to pay that 1/9d. a week for three whole years.

'We'll deliver it tomorrow,' said the ardent salesman. 'I'm sure you'll never regret it.'

'You don't know my old man,' I thought, as I left the shop.

Outside in the fresh air, and gradually coming to my senses, the thrill I had derived at the prospect of owning a brand new cabinet was somewhat dampened by the knowledge that I would have to break the news of my extravagance to John before the delivery van arrived next day.

I waited with baited breath for his return that evening. He was late. He arrived eventually, full of smiles and obviously in mellow mood. Before I could say anything more than 'Hello,' he was bursting with news.

'What do you think?' he asked.

'No idea,' I replied still awaiting a pause in which to convey my confession.

'You won't believe this, but I've just met Winston Churchill.'

'Winston Churchill?' I gasped. 'I thought he was helping to direct the war in London or on the Continent.'

'Well he isn't, and what's more, he was actually born in Dale Abbey.'

'Now you've got to be joking,' I remonstrated, wondering if perhaps I was not the only one of our partnership to have had a brainstorm.

'Well, before you think you've married a nutter, I must tell you that this particular Winston bears no real resemblance to THE GREAT MAN except in name and in the fact that both like to smoke a cigar — when our local Winston can afford one.'

'That's quite a relief, I thought perhaps you were going to ask the Politician here for tea!'

'On my visit to Dale today I met the man in question, and he told me that when he was born just after the turn of the century, as his surname was Churchill, one of his neighbours, known as 'Sandhole' Newton, suggested to his parents that they should call him Winston after the up and coming young man of the same name.'

'Very interesting,' I said, 'And now for my news.'

'Trouble?' asked John.

'I don't know yet — it's up to you.'

'Come on then, spill the beans, and if you've done anything rash, like forgetting to pass on a message, I'll spank you.'

'It's now or never, and to Hell with the consequences,' I thought as I began to relate the story of my shopping spree. I dropped the bombshell. John raised his usual deep-rooted objections. I countered with a promise to squeeze the instalments out of the housekeeping money, explaining that this new piece of furniture would not only provide excellent additional storage space, but would also help to fill up our jumbo sized kitchen. He acquiesced!

By stealth I managed to complete that purchase long before the Hire Purchase term expired. Later, emboldened by the successful experiment, I became by degrees the happy owner of an electric carpet sweeper, followed by a small washing machine, then an electric blanket, a new wireless set and lastly a refrigerator.

'Where there's a will there's a way,' was one of my dear old Grandma's pet sayings, but I feel credit for my exploits into the useful world of HP should go to the lady who originally filled me with extravagant inclinations — although she will never know it.

On the night of my confession, I retired to bed early. John was making a late night. I had had a very hectic day, and fell asleep in the middle of my nightly prayers which, for the sake of comfort, were always said, rightly or wrongly, after I popped into bed.

I cannot have been asleep very long when I awoke with a slight scream and a start. A strange, chilly feeling was in the air, and a strong breeze seemed to blow over my face, even though the windows and door were closed. I opened my eyes. At my bedside, bending slightly over me, was a tall grey-ish figure, madonna-like, with a voluminous cloak swirling around her. I blinked and blinked again. She was still there. Slowly she raised a finger to her lips as if telling me to be quiet. In fact, so scared was I by this time that I could not find strength to give voice even to a whisper.

'Now don't be daft,' I told myself, 'You must be dreaming.'

Again I blinked and rubbed my eyes, yet still she stood there, and, moving slowly towards the window, the apparition gradually dissolved into thin air.

'Thank God she's gone at last,' I said aloud.

I began to shiver and shake, telling myself that I really had not the slightest belief in ghosts, spooks or suchlike visions.

By this time, sleep and all thought of it deserted me. I tried to work out how such an unusual experience could happen. Perhaps it was some kind of optical illusion, shadows cast by the moon. But there was no moon. A nightmare, possibly? Reaction after my HP excitement? But why had the vision seemed so real? Could it be an unhappy spirit wishing to tell me somthing? I was not convinced that it was merely a figment of my imagination.

John came to bed in the small hours. I gave him details of my frightening experience.

'You're a bit over-tired, my dear,' was all the understanding or sympathy I received. 'You don't really believe in such silly twaddle as ghosts, do you?' and so saying he fell into a deep spectre-free sleep.

Never before, or since, have I had such a scarey few minutes, but the memory of that face, the swirl of cloak and wind, is as fresh each time it comes to my mind as when it actually occurred.

During conversation with my adjoining neighbour the following day, I described the ghostly happening.

'Oh yes,' she told me, 'I've seen it in my bedroom once or twice. You see someone was actually murdered in your house many years ago, and they say her spirit still walks around sometimes. But it's nothing to be afraid of, she's not violent, and she soon disappears — until next time.'

'Charming,' I said, 'I never believed in such things, but I'm not so sure now.'

'Perhaps I'm due for the next visitation,' said my cheerful friend. 'I'll let you know, and we can compare notes again.'

She also told me how she was just recovering from an illness affecting her chest and lungs, which had kept her in bed for more than three weeks. After giving me all the lurid details of her trouble, she ended with:-

'Do you know, Mrs. B., I've not BEEN for over a fortnight, and the doctor says if I don't GO tomorrow, he'll have to do something about it.'

I mentioned several means of relieving the situation, most of which she had already tried without success. Short of a dose of gunpowder, I told her I thought the Doctor should have acted sooner.

The next day she called round specially to tell me all was well, 'Mafeking has been relieved,' she said excitedly.

I suggested a daily dose of Epsom salts might ensure a non-recurrence of her trouble.

'I'm still feeling a bit under the weather,' she confided. 'Are you busy this afternoon?'

I had nothing arranged, the office was manned for two hours, so I agreed to accompany her.

'Where shall we go,' I asked as she appeared shortly after lunch.

'I'd love a walk round the Cemetery to cheer me up,' said she.

Now a graveyard, of all places as a morale booster, was not my idea of Heaven, but there's no accounting for the foibles of the human species, so I agreed.

We walked up the steep hill leading to the Church and its grounds, my friend's steps gathering momentum as we drew ever nearer to her idea of peace. At once, almost with gay abandon, she began to read one epitaph after another, at the same time giving me a potted history of the life and times of each poor departed soul resting there. More than an hour passed and still she was busily reading and recalling anecdotes, some of the more bizarre, I felt, embellished by her own profound imagination.

At long last I intimated that I must return home or the office would be unmanned and I would be in trouble. She straightened her back, heaved an enormous sigh, and together we retraced our steps.

As we parted at her garden gate she thanked me for my company, saying:-

'A pity we couldn't have stayed a bit longer. Still, we must do it again some time. You know we didn't see half the headstones.'

'A good idea,' I lied, thinking, 'Next time old dear you can take that particular safari on your 'tod.''

For myself, I would have preferred a sharp trek over our local Golf Course, or even a quick flip across the recreation ground. If it cheered the poor soul up a little, then the exercise must have been worth while.

CHAPTER 10

Doggies, Moggies and Other Dumb Friends

STRAY DOGS always caused me great concern, as also did the occasional lost cat or kitten, pigeon, budgie, or tortoise which arrived at our door, having lost its bearings, or suffered the awful experience of disownment.

Officially, dogs were the only animals we took possession of for the required period of seven days of care. Those poor little scraps, some mere skin and bone, sometimes mangey, mongrels usually, always pathetic little doggie souls, had often roamed the streets for days, weeks even, in fruitless search of home and food.

On arrival at the Office they were chained up in the yard, given a fresh bed of straw in the kennel provided, and regularly fed and watered by me. Sometimes we were unlucky enough to get a persistent yapper, but generally the strays were so grateful for a spot of care and a kind word that they settled down peacefully.

Our busiest time in this direction was several weeks after the Christmas season. Those once adorable little puppies who entered so many homes, quickly lost their attractive puppy ways in favour of hungry one-extra-mouth-to-feed member of the family for an already hard pressed Mum, and were cast out to fend for themselves.

As a lover of all animals, and in spite of lots of good advice from various people, I grew attached to each new temporary tenant of the kennel, and went out of my way to find homes for the unclaimed ones. If I failed, and regretfully I often did, then they were destined for a trip to HQ followed by sudden death by humane killer, ending up by being unsentimentally thrown on some local works furnace. I admit I wept many a silent tear as my here-today-gone-tomorrow lodgers were snatched away after their 'last supper' to a fate which none of them deserved.

One fortunate young dog, a beautiful Sealyham, perfect specimen of well groomed well bred dogdom, who occupied the kennel certainly did not come into the usual category.

He was brought in by a local young man who had found him in his garden, looking woebegone, lost and nervous. I was certain that before long the owner of such a lovely pet would be along shortly to claim him. I was not disappointed. Before nightfall, and looking extremely anxious, his owner arrived. As he entered the yard, the little quadruped nearly went mad with excitement, barking and wagging his little tail.

'You bad lad,' he scolded, turning to me, 'It's about the fifth time he's shot out through the garden gate. He's a proper roamer, but unfortunately he's got no bump of locality, and once away he forgets where he lives. We don't like to keep him chained up as we have a big garden where he ought to be happy running around.'

The pet duly handed over. Either he did mend his ways, or was kept under better supervision, for he did not pay us a return visit. Maybe he did not care very much for the scraps I had dished up for his dinner!

One morning, Elizabeth and I were busy in the kitchen, when a knock at the door revealed a dear old lady holding a very ordinary, terribly thin, tabby kitten in her arms.

'It's been around for a couple of weeks and nobody seems to own it,' she said.

'Sorry, my dear,' I informed her, 'But we don't take in stray cats. If we looked after everyone that is brought here, we should be snowed under with them.

What shall I do with it then?' she asked.

Whereupon my young daughter, up to now silent, yet having taken in the situation, interposed with:-

'My Daddy says we don't take moggies, only doggies.'

'Oh dear, I'll have to let it go then. I can't keep it myself. Can't afford to feed another mouth, but it does seem very cruel.'

'No, don't let it go,' said Elizabeth. 'Mrs. Smith next door says if you take it to the back of the Bank and drop it over the wall, Mrs. Bell will look after it. She's cat mad, my Dad says. She's got eleven and she won't even notice one more.'

Short of taking the advice of my enlightened offspring, I suggested the most humane procedure to save it more suffering, was to take it up the road to the resident Vet, as she felt unable to care for it herself. She left us, apparently undecided, but I had a shrewd suspicion that it was dropped gently over the Bank lady's wall to make number twelve.

Another moggie tale was unfolded one day as I walked into the grocer's store on the corner of our road. I noticed all the customers and staff were gazing across the floor in my direction. I followed the communal eyes down. There just by my feet was the large and lovely black furry green eyed monster, alias the Co-op. Cat. A still closer look revealed the reason all work had ceased for the moment. There, in the teeth-tight grip of the local predator was a very tiny grey mouse, who just managed to let out a terrified little squeak, a plea for help, I thought.

Where mice are concerned, I am not of the bravest, and my impulse was to jump on to the counter in case the scared little mousie should decide to take an escape route via my knicker leg. However, everybody else stood still, and I thought it best to conform, even though I was closest to the massacre about to take place.

As is the nature of all felines, Big Tim momentarily released his grip, letting the little mammal run a short distance away, then pouncing again, the mouse was re-clawed into captivity, unable to move, too petrified to open its eyes.

At last I could stand the suspense no longer. I opened the nearest door. Out shot cat with mouse hanging limply from the corners of old big mouth. In his surprise and haste, puss loosened his grip. As mousie shot off to the left, his would-be murderer turned right. That clever little scrap of vermin found shelter under a pile of cartons in the yard at the side of the shop. Puss, no doubt anxious for his crowd of spectators not to see his frustration at losing his pre-tea appetiser, stalked nonchalantly away, with an air of:-

'Not to worry — there's plenty more where he came from!'

'There's a pigeon on our roof,' said a little girl who called at the office on her way to school one morning.

'It's got two wings,' I told her, 'It will fly away when it's had a little rest.'

'My Mum said it won't, 'cos it's been there for days and days, and my Dad says to tell you you must come and fetch it down. He can't go right up there on a ladder 'cos it makes him dizzy, but he says your Bobbies don't mind where they go.'

That was news to me, but perhaps her parent had a point, although pigeons were not our responsibility, even tired or lost ones.

'Have you tried coaxing it down with some food, a few crumbs or oats or something,' I asked.

'Oh no, we daren't do that, 'cos our pussycat would soon get hold of it, and it might die. He's awful with birds. Do you know, he even chases the swans when they go for a little walk along the canal bank. But he hasn't caught one of those yet.'

'Well, well, we are in trouble, aren't we, ' I said, at the same time trying to find a solution to her problem. 'Tell you what, leave it there today, and call and let me know tomorrow if it's still up there, and I'll see what the Sergeant can do about it.'

She called later the same day.

'You know that pigeon,' she said, her expression quite worried.

I feared the worst.

'Well,' she continued, 'It's gone. But we don't know whether it's flown away or whether our Tiger has had it. You see my Daddy found some feathers on the garden path, and Tiger keeps licking his lips.'

'They usually fly away after a little rest,' I told her, in an effort to cheer her up.

But those tell-tale feathers, I felt almost certain, told their own sad story.

From time to time we were asked to give shelter to more unusual pets, lack of accommodation being our excuse for not accepting them.

A lady once brought along a tortoise which she had found wandering leisurely across the busy main road. That suicidal gasteropod was fortunate to be rescued, otherwise it would no doubt have ended its life under a 'bus or some other vehicle.

I informed her we could not possibly take it into care until claimed, if ever, and suggested she should put it in her own garden and make enquiries nearby of anyone who might have lost it.

She left, with tortoise, on her quest to find its owner.

'I've found the owner,' she said next day when she called at the office.

'Oh good, I'm so glad,' I said, always happy when the news was good.

'Trouble is,' she informed me, 'I took your advice and put it in our garden, and now we can't find it!'

Ah well, I did my best.

Here, my young daughter added her advice:-

'Tell her not to cry, 'cos my Daddy says there's plenty more tortoises in Derby Market!'

The resilience of children is at times nothing short of remarkable.

The larger varieties of animal life did not often give us much trouble by straying from the fields or enclosures in which they lived. We did, however, hear of one from a passer-by who reported having seen a very large carthorse clippety-clopping along Derby Road, with nobody in charge.

The morning was very dark and misty as John went up to investigate. Alas he arrived too late for, in the meantime, a 'bus conveying workers towards Derby had collided with the poor unfortunate animal which was lying lifeless at the side of the road with extensive injuries received by the blow.

John's first task was to get the deceased off the road as it was still a potential danger to other vehicular traffic. He invoked the aid of a local farmer, and with his tractor, the weighty body was moved to the grass verge.

The owner of the horse was contacted. He explained that although his hedges and fences round the field appeared to be in good order, sometimes a large animal, such as this one, would become restless, leaning or kicking against a weak spot, causing a gap through which they gained their freedom.

We all felt very sorry for the owner, a hard working farmer who had never been in any trouble with the Law. Not only did he lose a valuable working horse, but he also received a summons for allowing it to stray on the highway.

One of the most colourful characters I had the pleasure of knowing well was our local ageing Vet. I had met him some years earlier when he was attending to several of the Brewery dray horses, and he was always good for a few anecdotes concerning his profession.

It was, strangely enough, through a tiny mouse that we met again. I had seen the little varmint scampering out of the office into the yard. Anxious that it, or its family, should not stray over the border into the house, I decided to add a cat, or kitten, to our household.

I mentioned this to several friends, one of whom produced a lovely fluffy all white kitten, which we christened 'Bogey'.

In order to keep it 'off the tiles', and to protect the local females of the same species from too frequent periods of parenthood I decided to have it neutered.

Several weeks later, when it was considered old enough for the operation, I went along to the vet's surgery armed with young puss.

I was not exactly looking forward to the experience, but assumed I would be dismissed while the deed was done. Not a bit of it! Without asking me if I could stand the strain, the Vet. popped the front (head) end of the kitten into a small hessian bag, and performed the operation at the other end, as I was told to hold on tightly to bag and kitty. It all seemed rather brutal, but as there was not even a tiny squeak from that little victim, I assumed it must have been the usual procedure, and reasonably painless. Nevertheless, my opinion of that genial old gentleman did waver a little at the moment of incision!

With the approach of Christmas, poultry and pigs were always vulnerable as an attraction to the light fingered members of society. Although in our area we experienced comparatively little of this type of theft, arrangements were always made for patrols by regular officers and special constables to ensure as far as humanly possible that large, and smaller, stocks were safely locked and guarded.

The fox has always been a predatory menace to the farmer, but far more deadly at this season of the year was the 'Human Fox' — those Rhode Island Red robbers, the goose grabbers and turkey trotters, and pig pinchers alike, could prove far more hazardous than the four-legged beastie with the bushy tail, who prowled around during the rest of the year.

Regular visits and checks were made where it was known vulnerable stocks were situated. If anyone was caught 'loitering with intent' in the vicinity, he was duly summoned and fined for the offence.

One pre-Christmas day a report was received at the office that several chickens were missing from a garden shed. John and the duty Officer set about making enquiries at once, having had a discussion beforehand as to who, probably a local, was likely to be guilty of this type of theft.

One suspect stood out in their minds. They called at his house. The suspect opened the door. When questioned he flatly denied having been in the vicinity, and was in fact at home all the time listening to the wireless.

John glanced round the room in which the interview was taking place. (A habit of all experienced Policemen in search of clues). He cast his eyes over to the hearth rug. The feathers lying there certainly did not form part of the pattern on the rug. Several more were on the carpet, and that bloodstain stood out remarkably well on the pale fawn floor covering. Sergeant Sherlock Broughton was about to pounce.

'May we have a look round the house?' asked John, still not mentioning loose feathers and blood.

'I suppose so,' said the suspect, somewhat grudgingly, knowing that a refusal would have spelt guilt anyway.

Still more feather trail led the investigators to the bathroom. They opened the door, and there in full feather, well almost, awaiting the complete plucking process, were all the missing fowls.

'Where've you got these from then?' asked Sgt. B.

'Oh God, I might as well confess.'

'That was a lucky one,' said Constable to Sergeant, as they returned to base in order to type out the report on another crime solved.

'Yes, lucky I saw those loose feathers. They don't often come as easily as that one. Good for statistics, eh?'

Swans, gliding gracefully along the canal were a familiar sight to all our local residents. Often in pairs, and most years leading several cignets, they were a delight to see.

Intelligent birds that they are, they made regular calls at various houses situated near the towpath. The very first time I ever saw a swan on land, was one of our birds who regularly waddled along towards a particular house where they were sure of getting a few scraps of bread. I was told they even knocked on the side door with their beaks if there was no sign of their benefactor.

Just occasionally one of these beautiful birds would get into trouble, usually when in flight they managed to collide with a telephone or other aerial cable, or they got entangled with an angler's line, or swallowed a hook left carelessly in the vicinity. First aid rendered promptly by one of our Officers usually had the desired effect.

CHAPTER 11

Pyorrhoea, Agoraphobia, and the Little White Pill

I have heard of people taking up the Royal and Ancient Game of Golf for various reasons — post coronary therapy, the stresses and strains of modern living, or merely as a leisure time pursuit. I must be unique, for it was pyorrhoea, a goitre and agoraphobia which thrust me headlong into becoming addicted to the pivot and divot game.

Good health, as we all well know, is THE one of life's greatest blessings, for which so far none could be more grateful than John and I.

There are times in the lives of most folk, however, when a visit to the Dentist, for instance, becomes unavoidable, even though the majority of us, me included, have an innate dread of such encounters, being inclined to postpone the probing, drilling and needle treatment until the sheer agony of toothache drives us to his front door bell.

Since my early thirties, as a fairly regular visitor to the Dental Surgery, I had been fighting a losing battle against the dreaded pyorrhoea. Finally, for the benefit of my general health I was advised to have all my teeth extracted.

After two visits, each one paid with dread fears in my heart and mind, I emerged completely toothless, thankful to see the last of the offending molars and incisors, but scared stiff in case I met anyone who knew me on my way back to the Station.

Elizabeth was quite thrilled with my 'new look'. In fact I had to stop her saying to almost every caller:-

'Watch my Mummy give you her grannie smile.'

She even busied herself one day making me a set of orange peel teeth, 'to tide you over, Mum.'

Friends were very kind and sympathetic to me during my traumatic four week toothless era. 'They'll fit like gloves,' said one. 'You'll never regret it,' said another. One visitor was not quite so enthusiastic or convincing.

'It'll feel just as if you've got the piano keys stuffed in your mouth,' she told me, 'I know, because mine did.'

Four weeks to the day after the last offending trouble maker was extracted, I emerged from the first happy visit I had ever paid to a member of the profession, with a complete set of brand new dentures.

On arriving home I made straight for the mirror, and was somewhat chagrined as I smiled at my reflection. It didn't seem at all like me, although the Dentist had promised to copy as closely as possible the position of my own teeth. Instead of the usual four centre top incisors I had only two, and then the eye teeth were placed one on each side of them. The new set, however, included the four incisors, all fixed closely together, whereas my originals were well spaced.

I telephoned the Dentist explaining my disappointment. He told me that no dentist could ever, or would ever, want to copy teeth such as mine, because artificial ones in that formation would never stand up to the wear and tear required of them.

I retired to bed early that night, feeling quite upset at the fact that I would never feel quite the same as I did before losing my natural set. Sleep eluded me, with this result:-

Dentures by Design???

Until the age of thirty-three
My teeth were perfect as could be,
Then pyorrhoea began to play
Havoc with them, lack-a-day.

When those pearlies were extracted
Toothless me was quite distracted,
Perfect dentures in their place
Seemed somehow to change my face.

If modern teeth seen every day -
Too well spaced for the natural way -
Were set without such symmetry,
How much less obvious they would be.

Oh, would that somewhere I could get
False teeth to match my natural set,
Through them I would enabled be
To find lost personality!

Elizabeth, never losing an opportunity to drop a clanger, and anxious to show off my new teeth, remarked to one caller as she was about to leave:-

'Bet you haven't seen my Mum's new teeth.'

'No, dear, I didn't notice them.'

'Show them to her, Mum.'

Before I had time to give the lady my sweetest new smile, Junior added:-

'Do you know, my Daddy says Mum's teeth are like stars,'

'Does he now. Why?'

'Because they come out at night. Ha-Ha.'

So saying, my chick beat a hasty retreat — and so did I.

During my period of involuntary incarceration in the house, John had been taking part, when time allowed, in his favourite sport - Cricket. When he could get away, he played in one of the Police Teams.

Towards the late Summer of 1946, he returned home after playing in a Police Match, looking rather less than his triumphant embullient self.

'Had a good game?' I asked as usual.

'Mmmm, Yes thanks.'

'How many runs?'

'Fifty.'

'Excellent. How many wickets?' I then asked my all rounder.

'Three.'

'Not bad, not bad at all. You should be feeling pleased with yourself.'

'Well, I suppose I should, but I've been thinking.'

'Thinking?' I asked, rather surprised at his pensive mood.

'Yes, thinking, now I'm forty-four the time is coming fast when I shall have to give up cricket in favour of something a bit less energetic.'

'Why now? I should have thought that while you can score 50's you should stick to cricket.'

'Well, you see, I think it's better to quit soon rather than develop into an also-ran, so to speak.'

'Well then, what have you in mind? Bowls?' I asked.

'Don't think I'm quite ready for that yet.'

'Why not? Lots of young men and women play it these days. I might even join you — with a bit of persuasion.'

'No, not active enough.'

'Fishing then? But that's not at all active as far as I know?'

'Oh yes, plenty of Coppers, serving and retired do take up fishing, but somehow I can't really imagine myself sitting on a stool at the water's edge for hours on end, waiting for an unlikely nibble at the bait from an elusive member of the piscatorial species.'

'Good Lord, when did you swallow our dictionary?'

'Then that only just about leaves marbles.'

'Well, speaking of marbles, there's always the Golf Club up yonder,' said John, suddenly brightening up.

Here that particular conversation ended — for the time being at any rate.

It was by a strange coincidence, when John was chatting to an acquaintance at the local Conservative Club, that the subject of anno domini cropped up.

'I gave up Cricket some years ago, and took up Golf, and I've never regretted it,' said his friend.

'I've always thought of golf as a rather futile sort of game, chasing a little white ball for miles and tiring yourself out in the process,' said John.

'Obviously you've never tried it. Tell you what, why not join me at the Golf Club one day. You can have a walk round with me, and have a shot or two with my clubs to see how you go on. Anyone used to playing ball games, like you, should have a good start.'

'I'll think about it, and let you know,' said John rather half-heartedly.

We discussed the prospect at some length, and John came to the conclusion that a trial game might be a good idea, and a good way of spending the morning of his next rest day.

He telephoned his friend and fixed John's initiation for the following Wednesday.

It was a lovely sunny summer's morning when John left in the car to join forces with his friend on the first Tee.

He was missing for more than four hours. I had visions of him trekking over miles of scrubland which I had seen during my walks in the direction of the Golf Course, interspersed with small shapes of green sward with a hole placed somewhere near the centre of each, into which the players apparently vied with one another as to who could sink his ball first. Then I imagined him bashing at his ball as he tried to get it out of those deep sandy cavities placed at various strategic points all over the place. I felt certain he would be completely and unutterably bored with the whole exercise.

How mistaken I was! He arrived home eventually, full of excitement and, I suspected, a certain amount of beginner's luck. A full account of his game followed, as I listened in surprise.

'I did at least seven really good long distance shots, not always straight, but they even surprised my partner.' He said excitedly.

'Did you manage to hit that silly little white ball every time?'

'Well, no, to be quite honest, I did have a few fresh airs, as they call them when you miss it, but that's only to be expected from a beginner. That didn't put me off.'

'Don't tell me you really enjoyed the exercise,' I remarked, 'even after all your derision on the subject in the past.'

'I've just about said goodbye to cricket. I've never been so thrilled about any game in my whole life,' said Mr. Brimful of Enthusiasm. 'I hope you don't mind, but I've fixed another game for next rest day.'

'And the one after that, and the one after that?' I enquired, having heard something about golf widows in the past.

'You needn't feel left out. You and Elizabeth can always walk over the fields to meet us.'

'Charming,' I thought, saying: 'No thanks, I'd rather be the little woman waiting at home for your return.'

'I'll ignore that remark,' said John, not wishing to get into too deep an argument.

'I must try and get some clubs somewhere,' he said, 'Can't keep borrowing. It's not done, you know.'

Already he seemed to be getting entrenched in the etiquette of the game, so who was I to suggest that the money the equipment would consume might be used better to our mutual advantage.

With his usual luck, he saw an advertisement in the local newspaper giving details of a set of clubs for sale at 50/- (£2.50). Losing no time on such an important quest, he jumped in the car, arriving at the address almost breathless in case he had been forestalled. Dame fortune was with him all the way. The owner said he was the first caller, which was not really surprising, as the paper had only just been delivered.

He inspected the clubs, not really knowing a good one from a bad, and in his excitement quite forgot to follow his usual bargaining procedure when buying anything second-hand, by offering less than the advertised price. He gladly handed over the cash in exchange for clubs, a golf bag, and several balls which looked almost new.

He rushed home to show them to me. I thought they looked a bit antique, but held my tongue.

At once, out came the furniture polish, and in no time at all the two woods and four irons, all with old hickory shafts but like gold to his lordship, soon shone with the brilliance of a brand new set — well almost!

The clubs were ploughed (?) into service at the next game.

When he returned from safari No. 2, I made the usual enquiry.

'Fine, thanks, but those clubs are a bit on the old side. I'll have to swap them later on for some a bit more modern. They'll tide me over until I hear of some.'

Many games followed, sometimes good, sometimes a little disappointing, but my stalwart warrior battled on, his motto already being:-

'Forget the bad strokes. Concentrate on the good.'

One morning, when paying a routine visit to one of the local Pubs, his business finished, the conversation turned to his latest craze — GOLF.

'What sort of clubs have you got?' asked the Landlord.

'A rather ancient set I bought secondhand some weeks ago,' confessed John, 'Wish I could hear of some better ones, but they tell me they're very hard to come by these days.'

'Well now, the Wife and I've got two sets dangling from the garage roof. I can't see either of us playing any more. Would you be interested,?' he enquired.

'Oh yes,' said John, hoping if they were suitable the price would not prevent his acquiring the male set for himself.

'Half a sec., I'll go and fetch them.'

The clubs were produced. They were in near perfect condition.

'How much are you asking for them,' asked John tentatively.

Without stopping to think of any argument against his acquisition of two full sets of golf clubs, such as mortgaging the next month's pay, or even what the little non-golfing woman at home might say:

'How about a tenner for the lot?' asked the seller.

'It's a deal,' said excited John, 'I'll bring round the cash in a couple of days' time.'

'You might as well take them now,' said the ex-golfer, 'They're doing nothing here, and I don't suppose you'll vanish out of sight for the sake of a few £'s.'

Scarcely able to realise that such treasures were really all his very own, John was on the point of leaving the Pub, when the Landlord called him into his private room.

'Just a minute,' he said, 'I've got a few balls in a box in here.'

Whereupon he produced a shoe box containing at least thirty bright shining examples of those expensive, hard to come by, little white 'pills'.

'Here's a bit of divi. for you,' he said as he handed them over.

John brought his new-found treasures home.

'Two bags?' I asked, 'Whatever do you want two bags for?'

'How about you having a bash with the others some time.'

'Not a chance,' I said, 'For one thing I haven't the time, and in any case I've neither the energy nor the inclination. You know I've never been actively interested in any ball game.'

'Never mind, I shall probably advertise them, and they'll fetch more than I've given for both sets, probably,' said the undefeated enthusiast.

And that was that — or so we thought.

It is strange sometimes how an apparent quirk of fate can work out quite unexpectedly to one's advantage.

While John was enjoying his increasing prowess at the Great Game, I had not as yet succumbed to the 'golf widow' syndrome, and was reasonably happy to be busily engaged with things domestic during his long sojourns on little ball chase.

I did, however, notice one day quite a swelling in my neck, where a man's Adam's apple is fixed. After examining it myself about twenty times a day for more than a month, I thought it was growing larger. I decided it must be cancer, the worst. My days were numbered. In fact I worked myself up into such a state of nerves that I was afraid to leave the house on my own, and sometimes afraid to stay in it.

Every time I did summon up the courage to venture forth, my heart pounded, I felt sick, dizzy, faint and breathless, having to rush back to the security of home in case of complete collapse. Even when a knock came on the door, or the 'phone bell rang, I would break into a hot-cold sweat, having somehow to muster up sufficient willpower to speak to the caller.

This kind of behaviour was quite alien to my nature, yet I had no idea how to cope with it. Gradually the condition grew worse. I was in an absolute state of panic most of the daytime, and during all too often sleeplessness at night.

One morning, almost desperate, feeling depressed beyond endurance, and after inspecting my offending neck bulge from all angles, I braved the streets and took my worries to the Doctor.

'If I drop dead on the way,' I consoled myself, 'Someone will cope.'

The question was, could the Doctor do much to help me in my travail, as I had already convinced myself that he would shake his head and tell me I was quite beyond cure.

I entered his surgery, trembling visibly, and wondering how on earth I would have the strength to make the return walk home. I described my symptoms. He listened attentively, with knitted brow.

'When did you take to dentures?' he asked.

'About six months ago.'

What connection that experience could have with my present anxieties, I could not imagine.

'He felt all round my neck, and completed his routine general examination. He paused, wondering I was convinced how best to break the dread news to me.

'Now for it.' I thought, making a supreme effort to brace myself for the bad news. 'If it's my death sentence then I'll have to learn to live with it.'

The humour of that last thought did not occur to me until later.

'Now my dear,' he began, 'There's nothing at all wrong with you that a spot of iodine and some fresh air and exercise won't cure. You've got a touch of what we medical fellows call Agoraphobia, but I prefer not to scare my patients with such high sounding names for a complaint with which more people than we imagine are suffering today.'

'But what about the neck trouble?' I asked anxiously.

'Well yes, you've certainly got a spot of bother with your nerves, which has probably caused the over-active gland in your neck, (Derbyshire neck they call it round here). Lots of women around your age get some sort of trouble, and if they'd only come for advice instead of thinking the worst, they'd save themselves a lot of trouble.'

Already I felt much happier.

He went on to advise the use of iodised salt in cooking, which he assured me would not have any ill effects on the family.

'It'll do you a world of good, and won't do them any harm, shall we say.'

'Can you give me something to help these awful heeby-jeebies that attack me at all times.' I asked.

'You shouldn't need anything else in the way of physic, but if it will make you happy, I'll prescribe a mixture of Bismuth and Bromide, the Bismuth to settle your tum' and the Bromide to steady your pounding heart. But my best advice to you is to get out on to that Golf Course with your husband, learn to play the golf game, and forget all about yourself and your present apprehensions.'

What a wise man that GP was. He certainly hit the nail on the head. And get out on the potentially health-giving Golf Course was exactly what I did. Within a couple of weeks my troubles had gone with the wind — and that little white pill!

I could not get home fast enough to give John the great news, and the open air recipe for my cure.

'What a good thing I didn't decide to sell the lady's golf clubs,' he said, as he produced them from the cupboard on the landing.

Suddenly my apathetic stance towards the game which had already proved so addictive to John was transformed into an 'I can't wait to get going with it.'

John arranged for me to have a course of lessons with the Professional at the Club, and I then graduated to Sid Roper's Golf School in Nottingham. He put me through my paces, or I should say, swings, once weekly for several weeks, advising me not to play until my swing was well and truly 'grooved'.

In the meantime, the wife of John's first golfing friend decided to join me for a similar series of lessons.

Finally we both passed out with Sid's blessing. Our husbands were delighted. We fixed a foursome the following rest day.

We joined our husbands on the first tee, both determined to show off our lovely groovy swings to our men, and to anyone else who happened to be around at the time.

'You drive first,' said John, full of encouragement.

I tee-ed up my ball, with slightly shaking hands.

'Now go on, show us what you've learned,' said my friend's husband.

'Remember,' added John, 'Head down, a nice pivot and away it goes.'

'Wish they'd shut up,' I thought, trying desperately to concentrate on the essentials in order that the ball might go straight down the middle of the fairway.

I addressed the ball, and momentarily forgetting all the gen I had received from our Pro, from Sid and our two male partners, I took an almighty swipe, went completely off balance, and oh chagrin, there was that brand new snowy white ball still resting on its little wooden tee for all to see. I tried again, and just managed to scuttle the ball some thirty yards ahead.

John drove next — long, high and straight.

'Now show us what you can do,' said our male friend to his spouse, no doubt hoping she would do better than I.

She tee-ed up just as carefully as I had done, had a couple of swings, addressed the ball, and lackaday, she too dealt an all too powerful blow to our feminine pride. Her ball certainly left its little tee, but it forgot all about height and length, and just trundled forward not more than three yards.

Her husband's turn came, and we confessed later, we were both hoping he'd have a fresh air shot too, but his ball sallied forth to join John's right down the fairway.

As we walked forward to reconnect with our two unfriendly balls, John, by way of offering us a little consolation in our obvious distress, said:-

'Forget it, you'll do better next time. You've both developed lovely graceful swings.'

'What the Hell's the good of that if you can't hit the bloody ball,' said the other male member of the foursome. 'Waste of bloody money, all those lessons.'

I ventured to suggest that our men would be well advised to continue their game well ahead of us. Chivalry won, and we stuck together.

By degrees we both managed to control our nerves, and our game settled down after several holes of mediocre quality, and were even complimented by both our men on our potential towards the end of the game.

I can never over-emphasise the pleasure John and I derived from playing golf. When Elizabeth reached the age of eight, our very first set of secondhand clubs came into their own. Cut down to her size, she quickly managed to turn our duo into a threesome.

As a trio, we often spent the evenings playing several holes according to my energy and the time at our disposal. We played in rainstorms, hailstorms, snowstorms and thunderstorms, but I readily admit that at the first clap of thunder we were soon off the Course and heading for the safety of home or the Clubhouse.

One thing is certain. All work and no play was not in our book any more.

CHAPTER 12

Hail Peace — Farewell Ten Paces......

SINCE OUR ARRIVAL at Sandiacre Police Station, our part of the Country had been spared any major enemy attacks, although every branch of the Services was ever on the qui vive in case the Hitlerites turned their attention in our direction. By this I do not mean that the perils and dangers of war were not still with us, but we considered ourselves extremely fortunate in not being at the receiving end of any deadly missiles from the air.

At the Office we still received advance warnings by telephone of the approach of enemy aircraft. These, followed by Moanin' Minnie's warning notes, told us that a visit somewhere in England, however unwelcome, was imminent — fortunate for our area of course, but sadly they were en route for one or other of the larger towns and cities. We were ever thankful that our district escaped, comparatively unscathed, from the offending marauders, with only minor incidents for our local Services to cope with.

The wireless and newspapers kept us informed of the havoc wreaked in various places up and down the length and breadth of our Country. Often the period of awaiting news of relatives and friends who might have been injured or killed, was an aspect of war from which none of us could consider ourselves to be immune.

Conditions of austerity so far as rationing and other scarcities were concerned, were still very much with us. Christmas 1944 came and went. We had few luxuries but, like everyone else similarly deprived, we made the best of it. In fact, we were so used to wartime manoeuverings in kitchen, wardrobe and elsewhere, that it was difficult to imagine ever returning to the peace and plenty we formerly took so much for granted.

January 1945 saw the coal ration considerably reduced, coupled with frequent appeals to consumers to cut down on the use of gas and electricity.

The Ministry of Food did their best, not very successfully, to persuade us that dried eggs were even more nutritious than the shell variety. They certainly did fill the gap so far as cakes and puddings were concerned, but if you dared to fancy a boiled egg, then you'd had it, so to speak!

At that time my chick had no recollection of an egg locked in its airtight shell. Like most other children of her age, unless parents or friends kept poultry, she thought eggs came in neat little packets of yellow powder, which were invariably transformed into scrambled eggs on toast.

Similarly, a banana was but a picture in one of Elizabeth's toddler books describing the letter B. We did once receive an SOS by 'phone for a supply of bananas, which at that time had disappeared completely from the shops. One of the hospitals was in desperate need of some for the special treatment of a tiny baby, whose survival depended upon them.

John immediately contacted a local Wholesaler, who said he had some in his store and would be pleased to donate them towards the child's recovery. A quick dash by car by John to collect the life-saving precious fruit — a large bunch, more than sufficient for the infant's needs — then delivery to the

Hospital, was one of so many Good Samaritan acts performed by members of the Force. The little one made a splendid recovery, and was known thereafter as OUR BANANA BABE.

Time was when our purses, or at least their contents, governed our purchases. Now it was the RATION BOOK, our points and coupons, which had taken over from the family exchequer. Rations at this stage were at their lowest since hostilities began.

Each person received weekly only 2 ozs. of Tea, ½ lb. of Sugar, 1s.2d. worth (6p) of meat, (barely 1 lb. at the current prices), ½ lb. of fats, 3 ozs of cheese and 2 pints of milk. Points were used to obtain such rare luxuries as tinned fruits, jams and certain other goods when available.

People who were lucky enough to grow their own fruit devised many pet methods of sugar economy. In stewing acid fruits, the addition of bicarbonate of soda reduced the sugar requirement by half. Whenever two or more women got together, you could be sure of picking up some new wrinkle for extending the use of a scarce item.

The allocation of Clothing Coupons, 48 to last a whole year, seemed alarmingly inadequate, but with no alternative to careful scheming, we continued to spread them to best advantage by darning, patching, renovating and cutting down everything from clothing to household linen. With a modest hankie costing half a coupon, it was not surprising that many a shirt tail doubled up for a couple, or a tea towel even, thus saving precious coupons from being snipped away.

Soap rationing came as quite a blow to the usually super clean housewife, although no doubt this was welcomed by little boys who preferred the 'natural' look. Sweets, tobacco, cigarettes, cosmetics even, more often unavailable than not, became 'under the counter' products, or were reserved for regular customers only.

The 'wide' boys, or Black Market Spivs as they became known, made fortunes by selling, without coupons at exhorbitant prices, many commodities in short supply, including food, clothing, in fact anything they could lay their shifty hands upon.

This type of trading in our area did not come to light very often, but it was reputed to be widespread in towns and cities. Penalties for this operation were very severe, ranging from terms of imprisonment to very heavy fines. The guilty ones were fully aware of the risks involved, and considered themselves unlucky if caught in the act.

I remember searching round all the local shops, moving over to Ilkeston and Long Eaton, and finally to Derby, in frantic search for a pair of shoes for Elizabeth. In desperation, as the soles of her once good quality pair were about to dangle, I mentioned my plight to a friend.

'I've got a pair that my Jerry has outgrown. You can have them with pleasure, if they'll fit,' she said.

The idea of my youngster having to step into someone else's shoes, and a boy at that, did not appeal to me very much, but in those make-do days pride had to be put aside when the need was great.

I thanked her for the offer, and she promised to bring them round for a fitting the following day.

Elizabeth tried them on, and they fitted perfectly, and as they were almost new — the lad had outgrown them — I felt we were in luck.

Before I could ask how much I owed her, she said:-

'I don't want anything for them, you're welcome.'

I thanked her again, and was grateful for the coupons saved.

One of our regular evening pastimes, when all was quiet in the air, on the roads and in the Section, was to scan very carefully the miscellaneous sales columns in the local newspapers.

'Listen to this,' said John, during one of his scanning periods, 'It's under Articles for Sale.'

'I'm all ears. What now?'

'There's a lady's Harris Tweed winter coat for thirty-bob. Your's is a bit tatty, isn't it, and it says here it's for a 38" bust.'

He passed the paper over to me. I re-read the advert., and decided to track it down. After all, if it was in good condition, thirty-bob would not break the bank.

Without wasting another minute, I donned hat and coat and was on my way to the advertised address.

I knocked on the door. It was opened by a rather buxom (like me!) lady of around middle age.

'I've called about the coat you've advertised in tonight's paper,' I said, full of hope that it had not already been snapped up.

'Oh good,' said she, 'You're the first one to call. Come in.'

I tried on the garment, as she explained that she had made it herself from a length of tweed that had been in her possession since the beginning of the war. Unfortunately (for her) it had turned out rather too small on shoulders and hips. For me it was a perfect fit.

'It's an ill wind......' I thought, as I gladly handed over the cash. I could not at that moment have had a greater thrill if I had purchased a model garment from an exclusive store. How times can change our outlook!!

Elizabeth's clothes were always a problem, as she grew so fast at times it was difficult to keep pace with her needs. It was for ever a case of how to turn her out looking respectable and at the same time to keep within the coupon limits.

Several evenings after my coat experience, I noticed an advertisement in the paper's 'For Sale' column, for a whole range of outgrown garments to fit a child of Elizabeth's age. The address given was in Beeston, several miles from Sandiacre.

Forthwith I gathered up my chick and together we bussed it to Beeston.

We found the address without much difficulty. I waited with baited breath on the doorstep, hoping we had not been forestalled.

As the door opened, I blurted out:-

'I've come in answer to your advertisement,' as I hoped our journey would not prove abortive.

'My you're quick. I've only just read the advert. myself,' she replied. 'And you're in luck. No-one else has been yet.'

One by one the garments were tried on — little vests, slips, panties, dresses, two good coats, a rain mac, several pairs of socks, and two hats. All fitted Elizabeth perfectly.

'How marvellous,' I said, 'They might have been made for her. How much do I owe you for the lot?'

The figure I had in mind, hoping it would be far less, was around £10. I had grabbed this amount from the spare housekeeping cash reserve in the wardrobe before leaving home.

'Shall we say 25/- (£1.25)?'

I could scarcely believe my ears, for the total value, even at second hand rate, must have been well over even my estimate.

I gladly handed over the money. She parcelled up my bargain. We were about to leave when she said:-

'Just a minute. I've got a dress and a suit which I can't wear since my operation. You can have them if they'll fit you.'

She dashed upstairs and reappeared, holding the garments out for my inspection. They were in perfect condition. I tried them on. It really was my lucky day. They might have been made for me.

'How much?' I asked, trembling at the knees in case the price was beyond me.

Now either it was that I looked thoroughly down at heel and poverty stricken and she took pity on me, or whether she was just naturally one of nature's kind souls, I shall never know, but her reply really stunned me momentarily.

'Have them on me, love. I don't want anything for them.'

Overcome by such great generosity, I tried to press two Pound notes into her hand, but she refused to accept them.

'If they'll do you a bit of good, love, that's all that matters,' she said.

Elizabeth and I left her with grateful thanks, and I could not get home fast enough to relate our good fortune to John.

As I lay, rather restlessly, in bed that night, it occurred to me that if, before marriage, anyone had dared to suggest to me that five years hence my family and I would be wearing secondhand clothes, and actually getting a thrill from them, that I would be darning cuffs, elbows, collars of jumpers, cardigans and other apparel for the umpteenth time, picking out good pieces from a pair of John's trousers to make skirts for myself or junior, sticking bits of cardboard inside my shoes in an attempt, (not very successfully, I may add) to cover up holes in the soles, that I would be cutting down my own vests to child-size, laboriously sewing lengthening strips of contrasting material into Elizabeth's dresses as she grew upwards, I would have suggested they took a course of psychiatry as a cure for such ridiculous illusions!

Yet here was I actually enjoying my feats of ingenuity. It really did take a war to bring out our latent talents!

Throughout our deprivations, during the Spring of 1945 one bright star began to shine once more. The war news was improving day by day. The tide was turning, so we were told, and already hints of a possible ending of hostilities were dropped in various high, and lower, places.

With the prospect of bombings from the air unlikely, the black-out restrictions on our homes ended during April of that year. In May, petrol for private purposes was granted, although on a rationed and meagre basis, the price at the time being around 2/- a gallon (10p).

When eventually news was received of the capitulation, without strings, of Hitler and his wicked warmongers, we all nearly went mad. VE Day (Victory in Europe) had arrived, which meant that at least the war on our doorsteps was ended.

The fact that the other war in the Far East was still raging naturally did trouble us, but compared with the European conflict, it seemed far too remote to deter us from our own celebrations.

Countless private parties, street parties, dancing, singing and joviality everywhere were the order of the day. Scenes, such as had not been witnessed since the end of World War I were all around us. The tensions of wartime were swept away by each and every member of the community according to their lights.

Gradually our menfolk from the Armed Forces returned to 'Civvy Street', complete with their demob. suits, and any mementos they managed to pick up on their way home.

In spite of our relief as a result of VE Day, we were told repeatedly that there was no immediate prospect of a rapid return to normal supplies of food and other scarce items. Acceptance of the fact was not too frustrating, knowing as we all did that normality was bound to return sooner or later, but how soon or how late at that juncture was anybody's guess.

In August that year we decided to take a week's holiday one hundred miles away at ozone packed Skegness, the nearest coastal resort to home, shortage of petrol being our main reason for choosing this East Coast venue.

We were joined by two friends and their daughter who was two years older than Elizabeth.

In booking the accommodation at that particular time, when it seemed everyone was of the same mind, we found that the Guest House where we had stayed some years before was fully booked up. The Landlady, a homely person of middle age, in lending us a sympathetic ear, offered to help us out of our difficulty, if we would telephone her later.

I rang her at the appointed time. The news was good.

'I've rung one of my friends who does not normally take in visitors, but she's willing to make an exception for the six of you. She cannot cater for you, however, so I suggest you divide yourselves between her two spare bedrooms, and pop round the corner to my place for all your meals — and that includes breakfast,' was her welcome offer.

I gladly accepted her admirable suggestion, ignoring the possibility of any inconvenience to our party.

On arrival in Skegness, which was more thickly populated than we had ever known it in the past, we found scarcities almost everywhere, from beer to ice cream being in short supply. The only way to ensure getting a newspaper was for one of us, usually John, to dash round to the nearest shop before breakfast.

It was the shortage of beer, however, which almost ruined the holiday of our male friend, who apparently suffered from a permanent blotting-paper thirst. Most of his days and evenings were spent with a few minutes on the beach with the rest of us, followed by his lone tour of the licensed houses and clubs. Every queue, and there were many, outside such premises denoted that the tipple had been delivered and was about to be distributed among all and sundry, while stocks lasted.

The rest of our group, not being blessed, or rather cursed with an insatiable thirst, discovered other pastimes, such as sunning ourselves on the beach, bathing, walking, watching the ever popular Bowls enthusiasts, much more entertaining and less costly than our friend's persistent beer safari.

During our week in the town there was a great deal more than the usual excitement of a seaside holiday. We received news of the capitulation of Japan — VJ Day, as it became known, on August 14th. Everyone was almost speechless with relief and jubilation, most of us finding it almost impossible to believe that this really meant the end of all hostilities everywhere. Very soon the seafront was ablaze with bonfires, all went wild with joy, which was very unfortunate for our thirsty friend, for the Pubs were even more crowded than when we first arrived.

We returned home on the Saturday to the LAND OF PEACE AND PLENTY? Well, I really mean towards PLENTY by a process of gradual reorganisation. But who cared? It was PEACE AT LAST — the rest would come later — some of it much much later!

We wondered which of life's hitherto stringent economies would end first, next, and next, now the war was over.

Fashion, for instance, had taken a back seat in favour of standard utilitarian apparel for a very long time.

Now the Designers thought the time was right to put this right, to give us, and them, a boost, and in so doing to encourage the maximum use of cloth and other materials. Hence the 'New Look' was created, and widely acclaimed. Everywhere shop windows displayed this 'exciting new line', with its ankle length, fully pleated and gathered skirts and low waistlines. But, panic stations, we were all quick to discover that all the rest of our female gear, or most of it, was now démodé.

One afternoon, as I gazed with envy — and empty purse — into the windows of a local fashion house, inspiration brought forth this jingle:-

Fickle Fashion

A lady's waist
May change its place
According to fashion's
Mystique;
But men prefer
Her hour-glass look,
And static
This vital
Statistic!

It was not surprising that this new fashion, with its generally admitted unflattering lines, was short-lived. We soon returned to the far more attractive garments ending at mid-calf, or even shorter.

Peacetime and the relaxing of some of the rules was brought home to us, literally, one day towards the end of 1949, when we received official notice from the County Authorities that alterations to our premises, which had been postponed on account of the War, were being reconsidered. The changes would apply to both office and house.

In due course we received visits from various VIP's, including the Assistant Chief Constable, representatives of the Town Planning Board, and several lesser minions of the organisation.

The proposals included the demolition of the Loo at the end of the yard, together with the adjoining coalhouse, and the erection in their place of a garage.

On reading the blurb, I could not help wondering, 'Oh my goodness, when that happens I'll only have one Loo to choose from, and when the cell is out of bounds, it'll either be a dash over the road to the public convenience, (rats from the canal and all), or upstairs to Jeremiah.'

I voiced my apprehension in this connection to one of the architects.

'Worry not', he said consolingly, 'We're going to construct a toilet from a strip taken off the large and all too commodious back bedroom, then you'll be able to cross the Cell off your visiting list, and 'spend all your pennies' upstairs.'

I could hardly believe my ears, but refrained from getting too excited at the prospect of an inside Loo at last, in case the powers-that-be decided, when the estimates were received, that the expense connected with the new garage might not leave a big enough balance for the upstairs Loo.

My worries were without foundation. To our amazement and joy, work began within a month, and before long, oh joy oh rapture, we were all able to hold our private sessions in the comfort of home.

Sandiacre and happiness had always been synonymous to us since the day we took over at the Police Station, but the added pleasure of the County's latest construction for our personal convenience, was BLISS indeed!

Now OLD DEWDROP would really have to be pensioned off, or discarded for ever. Thrown with gay abandon into the dustbin? Not likely after such yeoman service. The sidebord then? Not very nice really after all..... Spring flowers? Just the thing, but what a pity to bury her pretty blue eyes under a mound of soil. Mustn't be too sentimental, though, but I do seem to be quite deeply affected by eyes of blue, otherwise I might not have fallen for John's limpid pools!

Daffodils, potted sunshine, nothing else would do. In due course that dear old Dewdrop was filled to capacity with bulbs, each one planted by me with all the care I could muster. My ecstasy, as a non-gardener, as those bulbs, every one of them, grew to maturity and a fine display of near perfect blooms, provided us all with sheer delight. Which only goes to prove that even the modest chamberpot, although deprived of the purpose for which it was designed, should never be cast away — by any member of the Force at least, for you never know when the next move may have its Loo ten paces, or even more, away from the home.

CHAPTER 13

Freedom Spells Country Cottage
and Oh No! — Not Another 10 Pace Trip

TIME PASSED so quickly and pleasantly in Sandiacre that by 1951 it was difficult to believe we had been in charge for seven whole years, and that I had been 'married to the Force,' for eleven.

John, a 'company's man if ever there was one,' had always been deeply engrossed in the job he loved, which claimed priority over all else. Now he felt the time was fast approaching when he should leave the 3-stripe tie in favour of something a little less demanding, with more freedom and regular daytime working hours.

We had of course discussed the question at length before making the final decision, but I tried sincerely not to influence him in any way. Naturally I looked forward to some future time when our night's rest would not be disturbed by members of the public who found themselves in various kinds of trouble and strife.

The total period of service up to retirement by a member of the Force can vary for a number of reasons. At that time, the minimum to qualify for the full Pension was twenty-five years. John's already amounted to twenty-six.

On the eve of retirement, a Policeman's main worry was to find a house suitable for his family, and by no means the least important — his pocket.

If, during our service we had been able to amass a nice big bank balance, this would have been an easy matter. Most Building Societies would have been more than willing to supply the bulk of the money. As it was, we dared not take the risk of sinking our very small sum, put by for a rainy day, into property. In any case, it was not enough to provide the full amount of deposit required for a house of quite modest proportions.

'Before giving my official request for retirement,' said John one evening as we discussed the prospect, 'I think I'll put out a few feelers, in case someone may know of a house to rent.'

'A brilliant idea,' I hastened to agree.

As usual, his luck was in. It was not long before one gentleman, whom he had met casually during the course of his duties, called at the Office. During conversation John mentioned his thoughts on retirement, and the difficulty in hearing of any house to rent, preferably somewhere in the Sandiacre area.

Imagine John's surprise when he heard:-

'Well now, I might have just the thing for you. One of my tenants in Stanton is moving today, and his place which is joined on to my house, will become vacant, and I haven't promised it to anyone else yet.'

He went on to explain that it was an older villa type of dwelling, and if we liked to pop up to view it the next morning, he would meet us there.

We arrived just after 9 a.m. and were taken into the garden first. John's sheer delight at seeing a very large plot of a size for which he always dreamed. In spite of its neglected appearance, knee-high weeds, rose trees that had long since returned to the briar, several very old fruit trees which appeared near dead through lack of attention, and other lesser drawbacks, I could see that already John had fallen for the place completely, that was before we had entered the house.

'It's just lovely,' said John, obviously very excited.

I added my praise, and hoped we would meet no snags.

'You've not seen it all yet,' he explained, as he led us right down to the bottom of the garden. There he pointed out the rest of our patch-to-be, (we hoped), showing us what appeared to be a mini-mountain miscellany of twitch, dog daisies, foxgloves and buttercups.

'Underneath all that', explained our host, 'is a lovely ornamental garden rockery which was laid out some years ago professionally at great expense. It's really only top weed, you'd soon clear it.'

'Gardens are all right,' I thought at this stage, 'But when are we going to see the house?'

I made a half turn backwards in an effort to persuade the men to forget the garden in favour of the building, when the landlord tugged at my arm:-

'Come here,' he said, and led us down to a rather eerie, roomy cave hewn out of the sandstone rocks in the hillside.

'We used this as an air raid shelter during the war,' he said, but if you come here it'll keep your butter nice and cool in summer, and make a good play room for your nipper and her young pals.'

I caught John's eyes glancing beyond the garden, cave and rockery. I followed his glance, and there just over the fence at the bottom of the garden was our beloved Golf Course, Holes 6, 7 and 8 clearly visible. What more could a couple of golfers require.

'But what sort of state would we find the house in?' I wondered. 'Perhaps a neglected garden didn't necessarily mean an equally love-starved house.'

At last our outside inspection was complete. We returned to the house, entering by the back door.

The kitchen was quite tiny, painted in dark green, which gave the impression of being drab and probably very damp. Under the window was a well worn sandstone sink. Five stone steps, also well worn from many years of downs and ups, were in the pantry.

The living room, with large sash window, was dark and dingy, the walls decorated with old dull paper, matched by the dark brown painted woodwork. An old cast iron kitchen range took up most of one wall.

'How is the water heated?' I asked, as there appeared to be no sign of a back boiler.

'Well, there's the boiler at the side of the fire,' he said, pointing to a brass tap attached to the side of the range. 'Or you just put a kettle on the gas cooker. You see there's no hot water laid on.'

'Charming,' I thought, 'I wonder what we do for a bath.'

The lounge, hall, landing and staircase were no better in appearance than we had already seen, as also were the two bedrooms. A bathroom? Yes, certainly, there was the bath placed near the centre of what had once been bedroom number 3, but it had only one cold tap and a waste pipe.

'No hot water?' I asked our guide.

'No, not yet, but I might consider getting it in for you but it won't be yet. You just have to get someone to carry up the hot water from downstairs.'

When I had assimilated that difficulty, I asked, tentatively:-

'Where's the toilet?'

'Oh that.'

'Oh that's outside, next to the coalhouse.'

'Now we have bought it,' I thought. 'Why oh why am I doomed to suffer such privation.' For I knew in my own mind that John would discount any objection I might put forward by the fact of the lovely garden to be and access to the Golf Course.

'Ah well, back to antiquity once more, and just as we've grown used to indoor sanitation, endless hot baths, etc.' I thought.

'Gas lighting?' I queried, as I noticed a grubby little shade on a central light.

'Yes, but I would have no objection to your putting in electricity at your own expense, of course.'

After climbing up a second flight of stairs, which bore the unmistable sign of that busy little boring weevil, woodworm, we arrived in the attic.

Having had no previous experience of woodworm, I felt very worried about its appearance here, thinking that eventually it would no doubt spread over to our own furniture.

We descended. I wondered what John's thoughts would be, but had no doubt he'd be in favour of taking over the tenancy.

'I'll show you the outbuildings, then you'll have seen the lot,' said the landlord.

There, in all its glory, adjoining a rather spacious coalhouse, stood the Loo, exactly ten paces from the back door. It seemed I was to be dogged for the rest of my life by the outside inconvenience of the essential convenience.

'What rent would you be asking,' queried John, rather apprehensively.

'Well, I thought perhaps nine bob (45p) a week wouldn't sting you too much. You'd be responsible for the Rates, of course, which don't amount to very much.'

John and I exchanged glances in amazement. All that for so little.

The landlord, sensing something was wrong, asked:-

'It doesn't appeal to you, then?'

John winked at me, and raised a thumb, I returned the signs. How could we possibly refuse, even with weeds, woodworm, and other snags.

John found his tongue at last.

'Appeal to us, I should think it jolly well does. We must thank you very much for offering us the tenancy. I can assure you we'll soon lick garden and house into shape.'

The deal was clinched. The key was handed over.

We arranged for a local contractor to install electricity, which he did for the whole house at a cost of £22.10.0 (£22.50) including power points where necessary.

A friend in Sandiacre downed tools elsewhere in order to redecorate the house throughout before we moved in.

Other potential improvements, such as the installation of hot and cold water in the bathroom and an indoor toilet, a new kitchen sink unit, the replacement of the old kitchen range, and many other minor alterations and improvements, we promised ourselves for later on, as and when the money was available.

All was well with our world. We could now look forward to the big move, as soon as John's permission to retire from the Force came through.

We were invited to several farewell parties, and on our last evening in Sandiacre, many friends called to wish us farewell. It was really a double celebration — John's fifty-third Birthday.

Removal day came at last. We all awoke early. The van arrived punctually at 9 a.m. All our belongings were neatly stowed inside. We all jumped into the car, and once more, followed the van.

Now we were off the beat, and going rapidly forward into retirement, and a future which we hoped would be as rosy as our past.